**Learning Resource Centre** **The College** of West Anglia

**Call 01553 815306** to renew your books or if you have any queries.

You can also renew or reserve books by going to
http://library.cwa.ac.uk/

The card holder is responsible for the safe keeping and return of this item. Fines will be charged on all late items.

D1464417

Camellias

DAVID TREHANE

Cassell

The Royal Horticultural Society

THE ROYAL HORTICULTURAL SOCIETY

Cassell Educational Limited
Villiers House, 41/47 Strand,
London WC2N 5JE
for the Royal Horticultural Society

First published 1980
Second edition 1985
Third edition, fully revised and reset 1991
Reprinted 1991

British Library Cataloguing in Publication Data

Trehane, David,
  Camellias. – 3rd ed.
  1. Gardens. Camellias
  I. Title II. Royal Horticultural Society III. Series
635.9′33166

  ISBN 0-304-31858-2

Photographs by David Trehane, Michael Warren and
  the Harry Smith Collection
Line drawings by Peter Mennim
Typset by Chapterhouse Ltd, Formby
Printed in Hong Kong by Wing King Tong Co. Ltd

Cover: 'Anticipation', a *williamsii* of columnar habit and with
a long flowering season, excellent for small gardens.
  Photograph by Michael Warren
p. 1: 'Muskoka', a good *williamsii* raised at Caerhays.
  Photograph by David Trehane
p. 2: 'Donation', first exhibited in 1941 and still the most
popular hardy camellia.
  Photograph by Michael Warren
Back cover: 'Margaret Davis', a sport of the old *japonica*
'Aspasia MacArthur' dating from 1850.
  Photograph by David Trehane

Contents

Introduction

Camellias are native to south-east Asia. Four thousand years ago the Chinese used leaves of *Camellia sinensis* for tea and the seeds of *C. oleifera* for the extraction of oil. Ornamental camellias were highly developed by A.D. 618–906, the period of the T'ang dynasty, and plants were traded extensively between China and Japan. The *Shorter Oxford Dictionary*, after the entry Cha, refers the reader to cuppa cha, slang for cup o'tea. Cuppa may be slang but ch'a is the old Chinese word, originally used for tea and later for camellias, which English sailors picked up when the British and Dutch East India Companies began trade with China in the seventeenth century.

The first dried specimens of camellias were sent from China to England in 1700. The plants were named after the German missionary botanist, Georg Joseph Kamel, who wrote in Latin later in the same year to an English naturalist, John Ray, and signed himself G-J-Camelus. John Ray, however, referred to him as Father Camellus and the Swedish botanist, Linnaeus, thinking him to be English, commemorated the work of this skilful priest in the Philippines by publishing the generic name *Camellia* in 1735. Hence the two pronunciations 'camellia' and 'cameelia'.

The great collectors of plants during the eighteenth and nineteenth centuries were surgeons and missionaries who relied largely on herbal remedies to keep their charges in good health or cure them. Botany was the handmaiden of medicine, for which the dried leaves and flowers were adequate and with which the botanical collector at home was content. John Cunningham, a surgeon of the English East India Company, sent home dried specimens of an ornamental variety of *Camellia japonica*, *C. sinensis*, the tea plant, and, strangely, *C. fraterna*, between 1700 and 1702. He was emulating, on the Chinese coast, what Engelbert Kaempfer, surgeon of the Dutch East India Company, had done ten years earlier on the coast of Japan where he collected dried specimens of wild *C. japonica*, *C. sasanqua*, and *C. sinensis*.

The Hon'ble Company (as it is called in the log of its ship, the Warren Hastings, commanded by Captain Rawes) and its Dutch

Opposite: the old *japonica* cultivar 'Elegans' has produced seven new sports this century

and Portugese counterparts brought into Europe, from the Orient, living plants of camellias from 1730 onwards. One of the oldest of these now is *C. japonica* 'Alba Plena', made famous by Dumas, which came from China in 1792. A hundred years later, nurserymen around Nantes were sending 100,000 blooms of it to Paris for New Year buttonholes (see p. 40).

The nearest the ship's log of the Warren Hastings gets to a mention of a camellia is 'goods belonging to officers of the Hon'ble Company'. Doubtless the camellia which bears his name and travelled with Captain Rawes from China in 1820 had its share of the 24,000 gallons of water loaded in barrels in the New Anchorage for the voyage home.

By 1830 numerous seedlings had been raised and the boom in camellias had begun. Alfred Chandler, nurseryman of Vauxhall, introduced his 'Elegans' in 1831, still a worthy camellia and still producing sports prominent among the novelties in the USA today – 'Elegans Splendor', 'Elegans Champagne'. Chandler and Booth published an illustrated volume with thirty coloured plates of *japonica* varieties and four of others.

The demand for more and more camellias spread across Europe through France, Italy, Spain and Portugal and to the United States of America but, about 1860, in all these countries and Japan, camellias went out of favour. This period of decline marks the dividing line between the old and the new camellias.

The old camellias were almost wholly derived from the species *C. japonica*. Coming from warm Canton in the 1730s, the first camellia of which there is any record in Britain was put into Lord Petre's vast range of greenhouses at Thorndon in Essex. The eighth Lord Petre was one of the most brilliant men of his day, not least as a collector and grower of plants. In his stove houses were pineapples, guavas, papaws, ginger and limes and, when he died suddenly of smallpox in 1742, leaving three daughters and a son only five months old, there were 219,925 trees and shrubs in his nurseries. This figure indicates the accuracy of his records, in which the botanists Peter Collinson and Philip Miller played a large part, but, alas, his library, catalogue, and botanical specimens were dispersed and, mostly, lost. Our knowledge of his *C. japonica* is, almost by chance, from a painting by George Edwards, in which he perched a pheasant upon a branch of the shrub and wrote (in his *Natural History of Birds*) that 'it was raised by the late curious and noble Lord Petre in his stoves at Thorndon Hall in Essex.' It was later said that the collapse of this greenhouse, exposing the plants to the harsh climate of East Anglia, demonstrated that camellias were hardy, although English writers as late as 1880 continued to refer to them as stove plants.

Camellia saluenensis (left), the source of hardiness for the *williamsii* hybrids; 'Debbie' (right), raised in New Zealand in 1965

A stove house was heated to 60°F (15.5°C) and it may be that this contributed much to the decline of camellias. From 1860 to 1910 great ranges of glasshouses were being constructed for wealthy industrialists and landowners. Camellias take up a lot of room and had to compete not only with exotic fruits but also with a vast number of tropical and semi-tropical plants crowding in from South Africa, Australia and South America.

In France and Italy new varieties continued to be introduced and it was partly due to the initiative of Henri Guichard of Nantes and his daughters Guichard Soeurs, who exhibited them at the international exhibition at Chelsea in 1912, that camellias began to shed their undeserved reputation for being tender and difficult.

The era of new camellias begins with the collection of seeds of *C. saluenensis* by George Forrest in Yunnan between 1917 and 1919. In 1930 the Royal Horticultural Society gave this species an Award of Merit. Mr J. C. Williams crossed it with *C. japonica*, and made the first of the *williamsii* hybrids. The two plants of *C. saluenensis* which he used still grow in the border alongside the entrance to Caerhays Castle in Cornwall. The hybrid which bears his name was given a First Class Certificate in 1942, followed by the Award of Garden Merit in 1949. This signifies that 'it should be excellent for ordinary garden decoration' – outdoor camellias had arrived.

Contemporary with this, Colonel Stephenson Clarke at Borde Hill in Sussex had crossed another form of the species with *C. japonica* 'Masayoshi' ('Donckelaeri'); the resultant 'Donation' became the best selling camellia in Britain.

The best of the *williamsii* hybrids have been bred in Australia and New Zealand, but our climate suits them better than any and in Britain the quality of their flowers is unsurpassed.

In 1932 that great propagator of new shrubs, C. J. Marchant, listed 12 camellias in his first catalogue. In 1954 he offered 83, and by the early 1960s Treseders of Truro were offering 310 named camellias.

This is not the whole story, merely the beginning of a chapter in which the other species, *C. reticulata*, *C. pitardii*, *C. sasanqua*, *C. oleifera*, and *C. cuspidata*, a neglected species, deserve mention. No less than 28 camellia species are now available in commerce and many more have been discovered in China, although they have not yet been distributed. The yellow-flowered *C. chrysantha* has flowered in cultivation in China, Japan, California and Australia and the flowers have been pollinated with enthusiasm more prodigious than productive! Visions of 4-inch (10 cm) yellow, orange, and peach camellia flowers have not yet been realised. The difficulty arises from the fact that the origins of the available yellow camellias, *C. chrysantha* and *C. euphlebia*, do not encourage compatibility with the species from which our cultivated camellias have been bred (see p. 44).

The excellent book *Camellias*, by Chang Hung Ta and Bruce Bartholomew, describes eleven yellow-flowered camellias. Ten of them are of a primitive type from semi-tropical areas of Vietnam and Guangxi province in China. The eleventh yellow camellia is *C. luteoflora*, which was found on November 13th 1981 by the Hejing Production Brigade at a fairly high altitude in Guizhou province, north of Yunnan from which *C. reticulata* comes. Not only does this imply considerable hardiness, but it is also more closely related to the species *japonica*, *saluenensis*, and *pitardii* so that, although its flowers are small, it may be the best source of yellow hybrids. It is not yet (1989) available outside China.

Where to grow camellias

CLIMATE

Camellias will grow and flower outdoors in the British Isles between the south coast and central Scotland. The choice of varieties is as limited in northern Ireland as it is in, perhaps, Perth. Provided the soil is acid, the limiting factor is the adequate ripening of the year's shoot growth and flower buds to withstand the winter frosts. Ripening is normally controlled by a combination of temperature and humidity, provided that the plants are being fed correctly.

Cornwall comes nearest to the ideal climate, with southern Ireland second, with damp sea breezes and enough sun to shepherd the flower buds through the winter but, even in such suitable climates, there are frost pockets in drowned valleys where flowers are all too often destroyed.

Shade is the best substitute for humidity. In the south-east, for instance, where the rainfall is low, summer heat is dry, and snow sneaks across from the continent at any time in winter, high shade from tall trees is invaluable. Tall Scots pines radiate a kindly warmth and provide acceptable humus.

Camellias may be expected to lose flower buds or, later, produce damaged flowers with black stamens, after the temperature has dropped below 12°F (– 11°C) for a few days. Young plants may be killed when frost lowers the air temperature below 3°F (– 16°C), and established plants cut to ground level. Roots are killed by much lighter frosts and, for this reason, it is essential to protect from frost any containers above ground.

Winters vary. In 1962/3 through some five weeks of continuous deep frost and snow the sun shone brilliantly, desiccating the evergreen leaves to death because no sap could rise to sustain them from the roots hard frozen in the ground. In these conditions a black polythene tent or an old-style tepee of straw or bracken might have saved many a camellia.

The 1978/9 winter did more damage in Cornwall. The unusual combination of a lower summer temperature, later warmth with rain, followed suddenly by hard frost intensified by violent east wind, proved fatal to many plants and defoliated camellias inland in some gardens even in shaded situations penetrable by this wind. It also caused bark-split due to the autumn failure of the ripening process.

In 1981/2 the winter was different again. Cornwall escaped unscathed but an intensely cold arctic air-stream swept down across the north-west, north Wales, Shropshire, the midlands, and central southern England as far south as the South Downs, subjecting these areas to a period of intense cold below the limits for camellias, bay and even privet, most of them cut to the ground and apparently dead. But it is rarely wise to assume that so vital a plant as a camellia has been killed and those bushes, apparently dead, which were given time, even until August, to shoot from the base, after which the tops were cut off, did so and were then helped by the mild winter of 1983/4 to make a good recovery. Some varieties suffered more than others, smaller plants more than large, and losses ranged from nil to 40%.

It has been wisely said that camellias can succeed on one site and fail half a mile away. Even in favourable areas there are unfavourable micro-climates – the dips in the road, the apparently warm wall in the bottom of a steeply sloping garden, which turn out to be frost pockets of unpredictable intensity.

Normal exposure to wind does little harm; the camellia reacts like any other evergreen with more compact growth. Obviously the big flowers, especially the pale ones, suffer in a gale simply by petals rubbing. However, a draught in a funnel under low trees or between walls or fences is anathema to camellias. The leaves become sparse and browned and the flowers are miserable.

It is worth remembering that frost intensity increases in proportion to wind velocity and evergreens on a wall in the path of a wind-frost may suffer doubly in the blow-back of the wind rebounding from the wall.

Generalising, it may be said that cultivation is most difficult in areas with low rainfall, moderate summer temperatures, and cold winters. Such an area runs south from the Scottish border east of the Pennines down to the river Ouse south of The Wash. There it is wise to seek out kind micro-climates – sheltered warm slopes under high trees or between houses where frost drains away, tree-lined areas by water which are not frost pockets, the angles of walls where shade for part of the day relieves the intensity of summer heat and winter cold. It is necessary also to practise every art of cultivation.

London and the big cities have a peculiar advantage now that they are 'smokeless'. The warmth from heated buildings gives London an advantage of 6°F (3.5°C).

Correlated with climate is the choice of camellias to grow outdoors. Generally the *recticulata* camellias require maximum ripening and above average winter temperatures, normally to be expected only in Cornwall and parts of London. The *japonica*

Japonica camellias, like 'Hagoromo' ('Magnoliiflora'), generally do better in southern Britain

camellias require fairly high summer temperatures to initiate their flower buds. In most of Scotland they can only manage a mis-shapen flower with few petals. The *williamsii* hybrids and allied hybrids with *saluenensis* blood can form flower buds at lower temperatures and are rapidly becoming the best choice for most of England and Wales, and central and northern Ireland, many of them flowering normally in Scotland at least so far north as Perth.

SOIL

Wild camellias grow mostly on slopes in woodland, forest, or thickets where the drainage is good, the shallow layer of soil is acid, and ample humus is provided by the annual leaf-fall from trees.

In small modern gardens these conditions have to be simulated if camellias are to succeed. Acidity may be indicated by the presence of other plants such as rhododendrons, heather with gorse, corn marigold, or spurrey. Lacking their guidance, test the soil with one of the cheap kits available. For camellias it should be acid in the range of pH 5.5 to 6.5. The symbol pH denotes the

'Leonard Messel', a particularly hardy hybrid, will succeed as far as north as Perth

chemical reaction of the soil just as °C or °F are symbols of temperature. A neutral soil is pH 7. Below 7 the soil is acid and above it alkaline.

Above pH 6.5, if the alkalinity is due to previously applied lime and not to the basic rock or subsoil below, the use of ferrous sulphate is advised to reduce the pH. This is cheaper than pure sulphur (which was recommended before), acts more quickly and reliably, and can be bought from garden centres. A detailed discussion in David Leach's *Rhododendrons of the World* (1962) indicates that to reduce the pH from 8 to 6 requires 18 lb of crude ferrous sulphate per 100 sq. ft, from 7.5 to 6 requires 16.5 lb, and from 7 to 6 requires 9.4 lb (8.5, 8 and 4.5 kg per 10 m²). Sprinkle the chemical over the soil, water it in and test the pH a few days later. If there is a risk of calcium being washed into the area from buildings, the vegetable garden or what not, spread a little ferrous sulphate around each year. Use only acidic fertilizers such as sulphate of ammonia and sulphate of potash and superphosphate or ammonium phosphate. The pH should not then rise because rain is normally acid at 5.75 pH (quite naturally and not by EEC decree!).

If the soil to be planted is raw, uncultivated or, for many years, neglected, it is a good plan to break it up the best part of a year before planting. This is when a heavy dressing of cow manure, a year old in the heap, can be used with advantage – to cultivate the soil as distinct from the plant.

The light acid soils of the Bagshot sand, stretching from Windsor almost to Weymouth, hot in summer, cold in winter, hold little moisture. Wild heathland when first broken up to make a garden is infertile. Digging in old cow manure below the top spit, after breaking up the iron pan or callus which is often in the second spit below, will establish beneficial bacteria and promote soil fertility, drainage, and water-holding capacity.

The heavier acid soils of Cornwall and Devon, where nutrients are leached out by heavy rainfall, and the stale compacted ground of old town gardens, especially London on its clay, benefit greatly from this treatment. If plenty of dung has been dug in during winter or spring, when the ground is forked over in the autumn for planting the improvement in colour, texture, and ease of handling will be noticeable enough to inspire in the most reluctant gardener a glimmer of an earthly paradise.

Humus is best provided by digging in coarse or medium Irish peat before planting and mulching annually (see p. 25).

Acid soils can also be improved by incorporating coarse acid grit or sand, provided the natural drainage is fast enough to prevent a planting hole from becoming a sump. Generally this rules out London clay, on which a raised bed is the answer, leaving the clay below accessible to the plant for water supply. A raised bed for one plant may be, say, 4 ft (1.2 m) square and 1½ to 2 ft (45–60 cm) deep surrounded by a dwarf wall which may be constructed of bricks, stone, concrete blocks or of peat blocks. These last have the advantage that they will provide a home for lowlier plants and look more natural (see figure 1).

Where the clay is alkaline, and also on chalk and limestone, it is necessary to provide acid compost for the camellia and also to

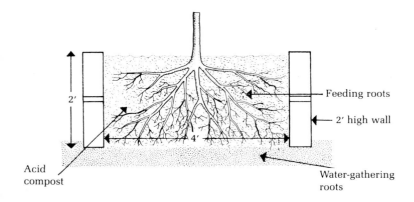

2′

Feeding roots

2′ high wall

4′

Acid compost

Water-gathering roots

Figure 1: a raised bed

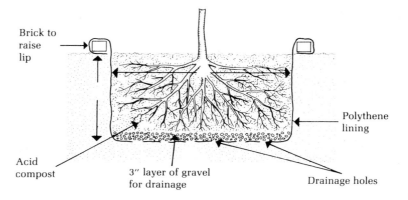

Figure 2: a hole lined with polythene

seal it off from the adjacent soil. Dig a hole, or raise a bed with walls, and seal it off with a polythene membrane of the type used for insulating floors in modern building construction. Fill with acid compost or coarse peat and sand; each plant will need a cubic yard (0.76 m³). The depth need not exceed 2 ft (60 cm). Drainage should be provided by making holes in the membrane at the bottom and covering them with a 3-inch (7.5 cm) layer of gravel rejects or stones, but not alkaline material (see figure 2).

There are areas where the pH is too low for camellias, causing them to make long branches barren of side shoots or flowers. Heathland in Dorset, Dartmoor above Bovey Tracy, and Bodmin Moor come to mind. The pH can be brought up by adding magnesium limestone, not chalk or ordinary lime.

Camellias are most adaptable plants, and, where amelioration of the soil is impracticable, can be grown in tubs or pots (see p. 33).

TOWN GARDENS

It used to be impossible to grow long-lived evergreens in towns because the leaves became coated with soot and ceased to function adequately. The clean air legislation, already referred to, has altered that, and the change to central heating has reduced not only the smoke but also the risk of frost damage, thus enabling hybrids of *C. reticulata*, such as 'Royalty', to be grown in London. The mixture of sun and shade derived from buildings and street trees creates an environment comparable with forest clearings. Provided care is taken to avoid the fierce draughts created by modern office blocks, and to ensure that the soil is acid, amply supplied with humus and kept moist, camellias, especially the whites and paler colours, do better in towns and cities than in more exposed situations.

However, avoid the temptation to plant nothing but camellias. The front garden with nothing but mown grass or paving, and camellias spaced equidistantly in circles of bare soil with no contrast, exemplifies the worst use of camellias. They like the companionship of other plants which shade their roots and make for a more humid atmosphere.

But it is unsafe to be dogmatic! I am often asked why a camellia, perhaps the other side of England, has yellowish leaves. Having eliminated virus I ask if it is in full sun. 'Yes, but the one next to it is quite green and healthy'. In full sun the roots cannot pump up water (containing nutrients) fast enough to enable the leaves to remain turgid and green and so to operate efficiently the growth processes and chemical changes which sustain the whole plant. The leaves turn olive green and central brown patches appear, growth is short and the bush becomes stunted with few or imperfect flowers. In maritime areas the air is normally damp enough to counteract this but not on an exposed south wall. I have a plant of the *reticulata* hybrid 'Dr Clifford Parks' on trial for training on such a wall. It trains beautifully but obviously cannot shade its own roots so the leaves are hard with brown patches of sun-scald, the flowers are few and short-lived, the petals soon wilt and

'Royalty' is one of the best *reticulata* hybrids for walls in London gardens

become brown. It is too large to move so I have put in front of it a *Pittosporum* 'James Stirling', with its small leaves spaced well apart on light branching, in the hope that it will filter the sun without blocking the view. It has to be watered too. The part-time shadow of a building would have done the trick in a town.

There is one exception. Autumn-flowering *sasanqua* camellias like a hot south wall. They have smaller leaves, are less prone to scorch, and need protection against autumn frosts, for their flowers, though plentiful, are simple and evanescent compared with *japonica* camellias, rather like shrub roses with hybrid teas. They are favourites in Australia for espalier work and fan out well on a wall. In London they should be ideal.

Old town gardens need thorough preparation of the soil which has probably had no manure since the days of horse-buses and crossing-sweepers. Plenty of humus should be mixed into the top spit, without bringing up the subsoil, and a regular generous mulch given with annual feeding. But cultivation in pots and tubs comes into its own in paved and terraced town gardens. One camelliaphile in London has over a hundred varieties on a flat roof, including 'Royalty', 'Dr Clifford Parks', and 'Lasca Beauty', all *reticulata* hybrids.

In towns too, there may be special opportunities for training camellias on walls. Most of the *japonica* varieties suited to this branch stiffly and have a style of growth which makes it difficult to stop them growing out a long way from the wall, so obstructing doors and windows. Some of the newer hybrids are more flexible but pruning immediately after flowering is vital. South-facing walls with midday shade, east walls with barriers against bitter east winds, and west walls (best of all) are excellent for camellias. For north walls some of the more graceful hybrids make a fine feature trained against them and freestanding the choice is wider (see p. 57 for recommended cultivars).

COUNTRY GARDENS

Assuming that there is more choice in planting than in a town, try to arrange for camellias to be placed in lateral shade, not overhead, unless any existing canopy is high. Avoid planting near shallow rooted trees like birches, beeches and other moisture robbers like privet. These usually win the competition for moisture; I have a large beech responsible for sudden deaths quite a long way from its trunk.

Near the sea and in the Lake District hybrid camellias may be grown in full sun and in the Windermere area are much superior to the old *japonicas* formerly planted there.

The fan-shaped growth of the hybrid 'Francie L.' (left) makes it ideal for training against a wall; 'E. G. Waterhouse' (right), a compact, upright *williamsii* hybrid

In country where the soil is naturally acid and organic, in the ordinary sense of the word, any garden will be the better for a liberal planting of woodland plants at all levels, trees, shrubs, bulbs and the little perennials which are so delightful and, perhaps, made the more so by the contrasting weight of the camellia foliage. How much more interesting the great Cornish gardens would be to ordinary gardeners if they incorporated the lowly plants which can be grown in smaller gardens. The art of gardening is the association of other plants with the greens of camellias and rhododendrons, blending the colours and forms of plants to complete the tapestry, creating unforgettable pictures.

The choice is enormous, choosing only plants which like the same soil, although in Cornwall it is not unusual to see roses and camellias in the same borders. At top levels there are the magnolias, *M. campbellii*, *M. sargentiana* and *M. mollicomata*, *Nothofagus*, *Davidia*, oaks and pines. At a lower level are dog-woods, stuartias, *Styrax*, *Parrotia*, *Nyssa*, *Halesia*, amelanchiers, *Oxydendron* and *Cercidiphyllum*. Shrubs include *Pieris*, azaleas, not forgetting the scent of the occidentale and viscosum groups, the swamp honeysuckle, *Rhododendron canadense* and *R. atlanticum* (for scent should play a big part in a woodland garden) zenobias, fothergillas, *Enkianthus*, kalmias of all kinds,

Leucothoe, Ledum, Vaccinium, Clethra, and *Mahonia.* At ground level there can be infinite variety – trilliums, erythroniums, *Kiren-geshoma,* ourisias, *Tricyrtis, Omphalodes,* anemones, scented *Smilacina* and lily-of-the-valley and *Cornus canadensis.*

Two practical points matter. Camellia roots run just below the surface of the ground and spread just beyond the leaf canopy. Some of these companion plants can stay put for ever, spreading with the camellia, but others may need dividing and they should be placed well clear of the camellia roots which should not be disturbed. Also any feeding of associated plants should be compatible with the feeding of the camellias.

SPACING

A plant of, say, 'Akashigata' ('Lady Clare') planted in a border 3 ft (90 cm) wide is soon going to overflow across the path. How often is this seen!

The information about the ultimate dimensions of varieties is scanty but, in recent years, camellias known to fit narrow spaces have become available. Most camellias grow to about 12 ft (3.6 m) high and wide and, when planted closer, grow into each other or require constant clipping. They can periodically be cut to the ground but they quickly refill the space. It is not unreasonable to plant them about 8 ft (2.4 m) apart, allowing the varieties room to show their qualities within a solid mass. Among the hybrids, 'Anticipation', in the twenty years of its commercial life, has kept its close erect form, staying bushy and floriferous down to the ground and no more than 3 ft (90 cm) wide. 'Spring Festival', a *cuspidata-japonica* hybrid with late small double pink flowers, grows narrowly upright but its habit is different, more like a lombardy poplar with laterals growing up alongside the main stem; if one of these tends to compete with the leader, it may bend out under the weight of flowers and have to be tied in like a juniper or cut out. 'E. G. Waterhouse' spreads about 4 to 6 ft (1.2–2 m) in a goblet shape. 'Alexander Hunter' branches differently in about the same space. 'Charles Colbert', 'Donation', and 'Inspiration' grow to a diameter of some 6 to 9 ft (1.8–2.7 m): 'Senorita', 'Free Style' and 'Wilamina' probably become the same size.

In the other direction spreading over a bank or rock outcrop, the traditional camellia for the purpose is known as 'Yoibijin' but correctly 'Taro-an'. 'Miss Universe' has a horizontal line and 'Mary Phoebe Taylor' is a spreader which, with a little persuasion, would drape a rock face. Among the *sasanquas* there is similar variation in habit, and there is one very narrow *reticulata*, 'Lisa Gael'.

Cultivation outdoors

CHOOSING PLANTS

A good plant should be sturdy and well-branched but it should not be straight from a greenhouse, over-fed, or soft. The woody stems should be brown and solid and the foliage should have a hardness which indicates well-ripened outdoor growth.

Small plants less than a foot (30 cm) high are almost certain to be glasshouse-grown. Such plants, bought in the spring, may survive in the south of England but from the midlands north into Scotland it is unwise to buy a plant less than 18 to 24 inches (45–60 cm) high. Such a plant will start off with more hard wood than the small plant will have by its next winter in the northern weather. Price increases in proportion to height but the extra is worthwhile.

It is obviously good practice, and attractive, to display uniform well-branched plants but it is irrelevant to future growth when planted out and could eliminate some good varieties which do not readily conform such as 'Cornish Snow', 'Elegant Beauty', 'Francie L' and 'Royalty'. Each variety has its own habit of growth which cannot be suppressed. The 'Adolphe Audusson' rigorously clipped in France, to get a bushy plant for sale, will straggle as soon as it is set free: it is its nature. 'Tomorrow' will, artistically, go off sideways. 'Tiffany' will sprawl. It is a natural feature of nearly all camellias that, be they ever so straggly when planted, they will branch out to cover and shade their own roots.

All camellias should be labelled with their names. The answer to a request for advice later on may depend on the name being known. Pictorial labels have their own problems. Some garden centres use bed labels, on a stem placed with a group of plants of the variety pictured on the label, and others have tag labels, one on each plant, showing a coloured picture of a flower on one side and cultural advice on the other.

It is essential that the flowers pictured were photographed outdoors in Britain. Taken in a hotter climate or a greenhouse, the shape may not be true to life outdoors in this country. Some colours are difficult to reproduce. It is fairly easy to get a bed label correct but it is not easy to get red camellias true to colour on plastic tag labels and they are liable to fade. Although the eye is attracted to the tag label, look for a decent bed label, which is more likely to give a true image of the camellia.

Utterly disregard one piece of advice which is sometimes given – that the camellia is an 'indoor-outdoor plant'! This is nonsense. A lot of painstaking effort has gone into securing for the camellia its rightful place as a hardy evergreen shrub, truthfully setting out its problems as well as its merits. Trying to give the camellia the image of a Belgian azalea has already done considerable harm and could destroy the camellia's future. Whether from a greenhouse, or not, every camellia for sale between September and May has come from a damp cool atmosphere to which it is naturally accustomed. Take it into the dry heat of a living-room and it will drop its leaves and perish. A modern home, constructed with whole-house heating to retain warmth and exclude condensation, cannot possibly provide a congenial environment. The warmth may stimulate the flowers buds to open; the dry heat will wither them in an hour or so. What is worse the plant will be stimulated into growth, which makes greater nonsense of the printed advice to enjoy the flowers indoors and then put the plant out in the garden. Once the whole metabolism of the plant has been upset by moving it into dry heat and its leaves have begun to drop, only a skilled gardener with a greenhouse is likely to be able to nurse it into condition for planting after all frosts are over. It is true that the official advice is to keep the plant in a cool room. The old baronial hall was cold enough but a modern small house has no such thing as a cool room.

The grower cannot have it both ways, nor can the buyer. A camellia can be bought as a house plant to give a short period of pleasure indoors, and then be thrown away like most cyclamen and other house plants, or it can be bought as a garden plant for long life or, better still in adverse climates, as a cold greenhouse plant. The one exception is the autumn-flowering *Camellia sasanqua* and its many varieties. They are bushy, flower well when young, like sun and a drier atmosphere and most of them are scented too. Their leaves are smaller than those of *C. japonica* and look well in a window.

If a plant has to be kept a while before planting out, bury the pot in the soil under a protective evergreen or move it in and out of a cold garage. Keep it cold but not frosted. Remember that it is the root system which must not get frozen.

For indoor decoration, it is best to cut individual blooms and float them in a shallow bowl of water. They look wonderful in a silver entrée dish, conforming to Mrs Beeton's dictum to keep the flowers low to facilitate conversation. A large vaseful of branches will generate its own damp atmosphere and enable the flowers to last two or three days, especially if put in the cool at night.

'Rubescens Major' is a reliable, bushy *japonica* cultivar for the open ground

PLANTING

The treatment of uncultivated soil has already been touched on (see p. 14). For autumn planting in an established garden it is an advantage to prepare the site during the summer when the soil crumbles more readily and peat can be more easily incorporated. A simple method is to mark out a square yard (or m²), spread coarse peat 3 inches (7.5 cm) deep over it, then dig out the top spit, mixing it with the peat in a heap alongside. Then break up the subsoil with a fork, replace the top spit, thereby completing the mixing in of the peat, level, and tread firm. Garden compost can be used instead of peat.

At planting time spread 4 oz (115 g) of John Innes base fertilizer over the area prepared, fork it in, tread lightly, and then take out a hole for the plant.

If the roots are all fibrous when the plant is knocked out of its pot, it may be dropped into a hole to fit it so that the pot soil surface is level with the firmed soil after treading lightly. Deep planting is fatal. The roots must only be covered by a mulch, not soil. Plant so that the finished soil level is at the same level as it was in the container.

If the plant is potbound and also has a thick dominant root circling the rootball, enlarge the planting hole so that the thick root can be disentangled and spread out in it, and then fill the soil in round the roots. Failure to do this may lead to root strangulation, the damage from which may not show until the plant is near

23

6 ft (2 m) high. Then the leaves turn yellow, and drop, and the plant tilts over because its anchorage is weak. If this occurs, verify the trouble by scraping around the base of the stem to feel for a thick smooth plate of hard wood blocking the supply channels and spread of the roots. The plant can be left tilted over for a season to encourage suckers to grow from the roots by-passing the strangulation, and, if they do, the old top can be cut off. This can only be effective if the camellia is not a grafted plant; normally only new cultivars and a few weak growers and *reticulata* camellias are grafted, and the union shows as a slight swelling just above ground level. If it does not sucker, dig out the plant and burn it.

Transplanting large plants

During the last century and early 1900s many large shrubs and maturing trees were dug by hand and moved on special horse-drawn carriages. Nowadays a mechanical shovel can dig a plant and drop it in its new hole in a few minutes if the site is accessible to the machine.

The more usual problem is moving a plant 4 to 5 ft (1.2–1.5 cm) high because of a change in the layout of the garden or a move of home. This is easily accomplished.

Make a nearly vertical cut with a spade all round just under the outer leaves in the autumn, after which the move can be made at any time before April. The difficult plant is one with only one or two thick roots and no cohesive rootball. In this case, and that of an old camellia, cut round in the spring to encourage fibrous roots to grow ready for lifting in the autumn. When transplanting, dig out a trench just outside the cut to the depth of the spade, to enable the rootball to be isolated, and undercut all round to get leverage.

A Cornish shovel with its long handle and V-shaped blade is excellent for the purpose! Tilt the rootball up on one side and slip under a thick polythene sheet; a large peat-bale wrapper is handy. Wiggle the whole rootball on to it. A fork stuck into the rootball will help and do no harm. Drag the plant on the sheet to its new site, make sure that it will be at the same depth, slide it in, pack it round with moist peat and fill in.

MAINTENANCE

Mulching

The word 'mulch' means 'soft', 'beginning to decay'. The *Oxford Dictionary* adds 'in gardening, a mixture of wet straw, leaves, loose earth etc. spread on the ground to protect the roots of newly planted trees etc.'

One correction is vital. Extra earth, loose or not, should never be spread over the root area of camellias. I have a plant of 'Julia Hamiter' discoloured and damaged for years by carelessly off-loading spare soil a few inches deep over its roots. The mulch should be an annual application in winter of a 2-inch (5 cm) layer of organic, well aerated material which will decay during the year – with the emphasis on 'aerated'. It should be the nearest one can get to forest leaf-fall. Bought materials help to prevent weed growth as well as keeping moisture and warmth in the soil. Ground fir-bark is ideal, sphagnum peat will do but is inclined to cake. Sawdust, wood shavings and chips are free of weed seeds and will last for more than a year, but they and fir-bark require extra nitrogen fertilizer to replace that used up by the bacteria in breaking down the woody material. Double the ration of sulphate of ammonia to 2 oz per sq. yd (68 g per m²) each year. Spent mushroom compost is marvellous mulching material but it contains lime or chalk, which makes it unsuitable for camellias.

Watering

For the first year or two after planting the roots spread slowly from the original pot compost and in very hot dry weather they cannot gather enough water from the small volume of soil occupied to maintain the growing head of leaves and flower buds.

It is vital to water well during spells of dry weather. In pro-longed dry weather do not let the mulch endow a false sense of security. It only slows down the rate of drying out, so check that the soil beneath remains damp. It is also easy to forget the effect of the plant's situation on the amount of rainfall it receives. Walls and eaves keep rain off plants growing against walls and the soil at the base of sunny walls dries up faster than the garden in general. There a trickle line, or seep-hose, is helpful. Hedges or trees nearby will rob a planted camellia of moisture.

Not only young camellias are harmed by dryness. It is the principal cause of failure in mature plants to form flower buds and, also, of winter bud drop. Rainwater is best for watering but an acid soil will stand several years of watering with hard tap water, especially if sulphate of ammonia is used as a fertilizer.

Feeding and hardiness

Camellias give a very generous return for annual feeding. Such a sumptuous array of flowers and foliage obviously demands it but so many gardeners, who feed their roses once a fortnight, expect a camellia to subsist on soil and peat alone. Peat does not supply

'Brigadoon' (left), an American *williamsii* hybrid which is very hardy and free-flowering; the *reticulata* hybrid 'Mandalay Queen' (right) can grow to a great size outdoors in Cornwall

fertilizer; it prepares the root system to receive it. The purpose of feeding is to encourage the growth of a healthy bush and the formation of flower buds, to develop the hardiness to withstand the winter and to open typical flowers in due season.

Most soils contain enough of the trace elements such as copper, zinc, manganese, molybdenum and iron, which are essential to the plant's health and the interaction of the main elements, nitrogen, phosphorus, potassium, calcium and magnesium.

Most fertilizers are sold with stated contents of N for nitrogen, P for phosphoric acid, and K for potassium (in percentages); one or two include magnesium, and, occasionally, the label gives details of the form of nitrogen, ammonia or nitrate. This sounds complicated but it is not really so, although the chemical reactions dependent on the form of these elements are.

The sap of camellias, like that of rhododendrons, must be acid. Hence the need for acid soil and, further, the need for fertilizers to have an acid reaction rather than an alkaline one in the soil and sap. The 'acidic' fertilizers contain ammonium nitrogen (sold separately as sulphate of ammonia and ammonium phosphate); phosphorus is contained in superphosphate and ammonium phosphate; potassium in sulphate of potash and magnesium in the sulphate (epsom salts) and oxide forms.

Unsuitable fertilizers are nitrogen fertilizers like Nitrochalk, potash nitrate, nitrate of soda, wood ashes, bone meal, and basic slag, all of which promote alkalinity.

Nitrogen is for growth, potash promotes the manufacture of food in healthy leaves, phosphate is for healthy roots and flowers and, with potash and magnesium, encourages ripening and hardiness.

The degree of hardiness of the individual plant depends largely on the time that growth starts to slow down before the winter, so allowing the wood and flower buds to ripen properly. Therefore nitrogen, which stimulates growth, should be given early in the year and it is conveniently done with a dressing of a compound fertilizer in March when the rain should percolate it throughout the root area. There is one reservation – if superphosphate is applied in June or July there must be enough nitrogen left in the soil to react with it and prevent it becoming toxic. Most of the commonly available compound fertilizers, such as Growmore, have an analysis around 7% N, 7% P and 7% K and this does not contain enough nitrogen to suit the camellia. So an additional dressing of sulphate of ammonia at 1 oz per sq. yd (32 g per m²) is put on in April when the lessening rainfull should not wash it out of the root area.

By the longest day in June it is usually possible to see if a plant is settling down to make flower buds. If it is not, it is helpful to give 1 oz of single superphosphate and 1 oz of epsom salts per sq. yd (32 g per m²), provided the nitrogen in the ground is adequate.

With such feeding, following the recommended preparation for planting, there should be no need to use Sequestrene. Sequestrene is not a food, it is a medicine or regulator of food, enabling a plant to use minerals in the soil otherwise not available. If the soil is acid, organic and well-fed, the plant should take up all the nutrients it needs.

There are one or two rules for applying fertilizer which must be obeyed. The first is that the soil should always be wet when the fertilizer is put on it. Sulphate of ammonia and ammonium nitrate are highly soluble and lethal if they stay concentrated among the surface roots. Neither should be put on in a dry period without remembering to keep the plant well watered subsequently. If this rule is not obeyed the leaves will go brown and curl up; a young plant will die very quickly.

The second is that the fertilizer should be sprinkled evenly over the root area, which normally extends from, say, 6 or 12 inches (15–30 cm) from the main stem, according to its age, to, say, 6 or 9 inches (15–23 cm) beyond the leaf-spread. If any falls on the leaves it should be washed off.

The third is that if the John Innes base fertilizer has been used in the planting hole, no more fertilizer should be given during the first year of growth (see p. 23).

Finally, no fertilizer should be given after the end of June, as it delays the essential ripening of the wood.

The use of animal manures is controversial. Recommendations vary from the use of well-rotted cow dung chopped up with peat or straw as a mulch, to well-rotted manure dug in 2 ft (60 cm) down before planting. The quality of farmyard manure is variable, as is the interpretation of the expression 'well-rotted'. The texture of cow dung is the antithesis of the well-aerated soil needed for camellias. Dung has the further drawback of releasing chemicals and gases irregularly and at the wrong time of the year. Having seen many brown-edged leaves owing their disfigurement and premature fall to animal manure, I am wholly opposed to its use for camellias, as distinct from its use in the preparation of the bare soil many months ahead of planting. A peat and fertilizer regime is much safer.

But time does not stand still! The changes from soggy farmyard manure by the load to a dried graded product sold by the bag, with an analysis, is accelerating. Blended mixtures of dried cow manure and peat, contrived for rhododendrons and camellias, are becoming available and these may well be excellent for a combined mulch and feed.

Weeds

The traditional weedkiller is the hoe, in this case, preferably, a Dutch hoe which cannot go deep enough to damage the roots which are usually near the surface in Britain. Deep cultivation of camellias should always be avoided.

If camellias are mulched regularly, weeds should not be a problem and nothing is better for them than a good layer of peat or ground fir-bark. It is, however, expensive unless it saves the wages of a gardener, to mulch large areas between plants 8 ft (2.4 m) apart.

Chemical weedkillers are available for both the prevention and control of weeds. Seedling weeds can be prevented by using simazine (as directed on the container) on clean weed-free ground. Moss alone will grow.

Annual weeds can be killed with paraquat with diquat but the smallest drop on green tissue will kill it, so special care should be taken to avoid spray drift or splash on to leaves of the camellias. Glyphosate will kill (much more slowly) annual and most perennial weeds too, but great care should be taken to avoid spray drift. Its best use is in the preparation of a site, clearing it of couch and nettles. Alloxydim sodium is also effective against couch and most perennial grasses, and harmless to non-grassy plants.

PRUNING

The idea of cutting a camellia causes more apprehension than almost any other aspect of its cultivation. It need not. The camellia can be treated like a laurel, except that one has to encourage flower buds. When cutting for the house, do not prune back to a main stem but to a side shoot, which will probably give flowers the following spring.

A dense rounded bush needs no pruning, but irregular long shoots, making a young plant lop-sided, should be cut back in winter. Once a balanced bush has been formed, the occasional erratic shoot is better cut back, or right out, immediately after flowering, the latest time for pruning.

Cutting back into old wood in spring delays growth for about 5 weeks and may upset the plant's initiation of flower buds.

An old overgrown bush, still healthy, may safely be cut down close to ground level and will bush out better than one cut half way or to knee height. Be quite fearless about this even at the risk of domestic strife. Paint any large cuts with a wound sealant to prevent decay. If the old bush is a grafted plant cut to a foot (30 cm) high and watch for suckers which will almost certainly have different leaves. These should be pulled, not cut, off.

Camellias trained on walls require pruning each spring. The process varies according to each variety's type of growth. The aim is to keep the growth as tight to the wall as possible without diminishing the display of flowers. Start working on a bush as soon as it begins to go out of flower, pruning back each shoot in turn. Beyond the flowers on a lateral branch there will usually be a new terminal shoot starting into growth, perhaps a smaller one behind it and, nearest the wall, a rosette of leaves, or a short shoot emerging. Cut back to the rosette or short shoot. Sometimes one has to cut back to just a leaf and hope that new growth will grow from its axillary bud. If strong growths appear where they are not wanted, cut them right out. If they fit in but need slowing down, pinch out their soft tips during the growing season to make them branch and to keep them within bounds.

Hedges

Camellias clipped to form hedges and topiary abound in Spain and Portugal. Mine is of 'Tiptoe', using up old leggy reject plants 18 inches (45 cm) high planted $2\frac{1}{2}$ feet (75 cm) apart. They have made a hedge so dense and uniform that, after some ten or more years, they have needed no clipping. This camellia is ideal except that, being a second generation *williamsii* hybrid, its semi-double pink flowers do not drop; they have to be shaken quite hard and

Camellia japonica 'Tricolor', a popular striped camellia with wavy leaves

the odd ones left on have to be picked off. I know no camellia equally twiggy which sheds its flowers except 'Spring Festival', which has a different type of growth, very tight but with ascending branches. Occasionally a branch will fall outwards with the weight of flowers. It can be tied back in or cut right out. The best recommendations I can make for camellias which grow closely enough to need no clipping for many years are 'Charles Colbert', 'Commander Mulroy', 'Janet Waterhouse', 'Senorita', 'Spring Festival', and, perhaps, 'Alexander Hunter'. In a small space these varieties will eventually require annual clipping, which should always be done immediately after flowering.

Do not be tempted to buy for a hedge large plants 'because camellias are so slow'. As with yew, a small plant treated well will soon overtake a larger one from open ground.

Grooming and disbudding

Most *japonica* camellias do not shed dead flowers so that these when brown look unsightly. Most spent flowers can be dislodged by tapping the branches sharply with a stick.

The *sasanquas*, *reticulatas*, and many of the *williamsii* hybrids do drop flowers, or they shatter, when over. Frosted flowers stay on and must be tapped or shaken off.

Many camellias form clusters of flower buds. Many of the most immature will drop off after the first frost. The rest can safely be left on even the smallest plant without overtaxing it. If show flowers are required, disbudding to a single bud is necessary.

Cultivation under cover

The flowers of most *japonica* camellias, particularly white and pale pinks, are finer in cold greenhouses which give protection from wind and frost at flowering time. Except for favoured areas like Cornwall, the flamboyant *reticulata* camellias and *C. granthamiana* must be grown in a greenhouse, where they will make a fabulous display. Many of the other species with small dainty flowers, and their hybrids, are essentially greenhouse plants. Certainly the yellow camellias, *C. chrysantha* and *C. euphlebia* are. Scented camellias give their full value only under cover. 'Flower Girl', 'Dream Girl', and 'Show Girl', which flower in midwinter, although fully hardy, spread their fragrance only in a confined space. It is only under glass, when the temperature reaches 60°F (15.5°C) or so that the sweet scent of 'Kramer's Supreme' and *C. lutchuensis* hybrids like 'Fragrant Pink' and 'Spring Mist' can be sensed and enjoyed.

The flowers of some camellias show a different form in the greenhouse. Those of 'Laurie Bray' and 'Leonard Messel', for example, are loose peony form outdoors but under glass they are semi-double (see p. 50). Some peony form flowers have more regular and rounded form outdoors than under glass, where the extra warmth makes petals proliferate to the point of unsightly congestion. Similarly the anemone form flowers of 'Laura Boscawen' and 'Jury's Yellow' are more compact and well-defined outdoors. Indeed, generally, the hybrids with *saluenensis*, especially the *williamsii* hybrids such as 'Dream Boat', 'Water Lily', and 'Anticipation', produce better quality flowers outdoors and they grow better there too. The flowers enjoy low temperatures, only just above freezing, a minimum of 40°F (4.5°C), so there is no need to waste heat.

In large greenhouses camellias can be planted in the ground. Many of the species are small trees in the wild and, like *C. tsaii* and *C. taliensis*, flower in winter, making good use of head-room. Inevitably a large collection will be planted closely. One collection I know includes the 'Elegans' group housed in pots placed close together and taken up the side of a small greenhouse, like single cordons, very successfully. (For growing in containers, see p. 33).

After flowering, priority should be given to a methodical pruning of the plants, back to side shoots to keep them within bounds. The same sort of pruning is done in the USA to get show

'Mrs D. W. Davis' produces enormous blooms under glass

flowers, thinning out growths to give each selected flower bud 9 inches (23 cm) of clear space. To prevent rubbing of petals adjacent stems can be held back with clothes pegs.

Camellias flower when little else in the garden is producing nectar and small birds may have to be excluded by netting ventilators and doorways. Camellias also grow earlier under protection and control of aphids on the succulent young shoots is essential (see p. 61).

It is common practice to move camellias in pots out of the greenhouse after flowering to make room for other plants. But remember that soft growth starts before flowering is over and can be sharply blackened by frost. A sheltered but not draughty place should be chosen for the summer standing ground and, if used before frosts are past, a temporary cover should be rigged. Frosting of young shoots sets the plants back some weeks and may prejudice the formation of flower buds.

Provided pots are plunged or otherwise protected, they can be left outdoors in the winter until near flowering time if the greenhouse is wanted for chrysanthemums.

Camellias in containers

Although camellias in the ground have shallow spreading roots, they grow remarkably well in pots, tubs, urns, and the like. Plants 5 ft (1.5 m) high or more will flourish in 10-inch (25 cm) pots for many years and demand no special skill from their owner.

In greenhouses the use of containers enables a large collection to be grown, and changed, in a small space and allows that small space to be put to maximum use.

Outdoors camellias in ornamental containers, or in purpose-made recesses, on patios and terraces, make admirable accent plants. The use of containers also overcomes the problem of adverse garden soil.

There is one cardinal rule which is absolutely vital. Camellias in pots, or any other container, must never be allowed to have their roots frozen through. If the soil in the container freezes solid, the roots die. Whatever the weather prophets say, it must be a routine measure to insulate the pots with straw, bracken, woodwool, sawdust, whatever is available, in the autumn. Polystyrene granules as used for packing are excellent, since they are clean, warm, and drain well.

COMPOST

Camellia plants sold in pots are either in a loam-based compost – a mixture of loam, peat, sand – or in a peat-sand mix.

The loam-based compost has three advantages. It is heavier and therefore gives greater stability to top-heavy plants. The loam supplies trace elements, which usually have to be added to peat-sand mixes. A loam-based compost is easier to water.

The standard loam-based John Innes (JI) compost contains chalk and camellias, except C. sasanqua, are recognised as calcifuge shrubs. It is therefore necessary when buying compost to ask for JI potting compost No. 1, 2 or 3 without chalk, to be made up and supplied. JI No. 1 is for small plants, up to No. 3 for large (the fertilizer content is increased with the number).

The best advice for making JI compost is to use acid loam if available, neutral if not, and to omit the chalk. The formula for the potting compost is 7 parts by loose bulk of medium loam, 3 of medium grade moss-peat, 2 of coarse (acid) sand, adding for JI No. 1 the JI base fertilizer at 4 oz (113 g) to a bushel (36.3 litres) of the mixture, 8 oz (227 g) for No. 2 and 12 oz (340 g) for No. 3. This will then keep for two months. Loam should ideally be sterilised.

The alternative to a JI compost is a mixture of peat and sand, generally sold as ericaceous compost or rhododendron compost, and preferably one *without* a wetter. This should have the correct pH, the essential trace elements and enough nitrogen, phosphate and potash to last for some six weeks. After this period strong growing plants will require feeding. In almost standard commercial use is a compost containing fairly finely ground bark. This may require trace elements or they may be already included, and it incorporates slow-release fertilizers.

The soil-less composts are very pleasant to handle but they require careful management, must not be over-firmed or allowed to dry out and the extra feeding should not be erratic but carefully timed to follow the life of the fertilizers.

POTTING ON

A bought plant 18 to 24 inches (45–60 cm) high in a 5-inch (12.5 cm) pot will generally need potting on into a larger container. If in doubt turn the plant upside down and tap it out of the pot. If few roots are visible it will stand another year with feeding. If there is a tight ball of roots it must be potted on. Traditionally camellias have been potted on into a pot 2 inches (5 cm) wider – 5 to 7, 7 to 9 and so on, to the final size.

Similarly it has been recommended that, instead of moving it straight from a 5-inch (12.5 cm) pot into a large urn or tub, a camellia should be potted on into a 7-inch (18 cm) and plunged in soil or sand in the urn. The reason given was that this was to prevent the large volume of unoccupied compost going 'sour'. There is no recorded research on this and there must be many camellias which have been safely grown with just the one move from a small pot into a large container. The essential appears to be that the compost is free draining.

In potting on, compost is put in the bottom of a larger container, the plant stood on it, compost heaped over its roots, the pot tapped on the bench to shake the compost together, topped up and then pressed down the side of the pot with the finger-tips, topping up again if necessary and tapping to level down so that the new compost is only just covering the rootball. On no account should the new compost be firmed solidly with a rammer. Camellia roots spread best in fairly loose compost akin to forest soil.

The top of the compost in a 10-inch (25 cm) pot should be 1½ inches (4 cm) below the rim to allow room for watering.

'Dr Burnside' is a fine *japonica* cultivar for growing in a container

RE-POTTING

When a camellia has been put into its final container some natural shrinkage of the compost will occur each year and this can be made up in late winter with a top-dressing of new compost containing a high level of fertilizer.

The time for more drastic action comes when normal feeding fails to keep the good colour of the leaves, the quality of the flowers and their stems. Camellias are very tough and forbearing but when they go beyond their limit they decline very rapidly and restoration is a slow process.

The same container can be used, after cleaning. The procedure is to take the plant out of the container, brutally if necessary, and then to rub or comb off an inch (2.5 cm) or two of the root-ball all round the sides and shoulders, and tear or cut 2 inches (5 cm) or more off the bottom and tease out the ends of the roots exposed. A layer of fresh compost is then put into the bottom of the container, the plant put back and filled in round as for potting on, shaking the plant as much as possible so that the compost is worked in among the roots and no air pockets remain.

WATERING

After re-potting, water in once and then take care not to kill the camellia by over-watering. Damping over will probably be

35

enough until new roots have grown. Correct watering is a matter of observation and getting the feel of the plant! Modern gadgets to indicate the need for water do not entirely take the place of sound judgement. In the commuter's fully automatic greenhouse it can be left to the electronics along with the heat, shading, ventilation, feeding and humidifiers but it is still worth checking how plants in the back row compare with the rest.

The type of container affects the demand for water. If a plastic pot requires water every three days, a clay pot will need it every two. The amount of leaf affects the demand. *Reticulata* camellias take less water than *japonicas*.

When watering with a hose the top compost is liable to be washed out of the pot. A layer of pebbles will prevent this.

Extremes should be avoided in watering camellias. Generally a plant left to get very dry will recover after a soaking, but it may lose its flower buds. Over-watering until leaves have yellowed and begun to drop is usually fatal. By that time the roots have rotted. The natural tendency to over-water has to be curbed.

Most mains water is deliberately hardened, some is naturally very hard, and this may be a problem when plants are in containers. Although there is a natural process of acidification going on in the compost, the volume of compost is small compared with soil around a camellia planted outdoors.

The simplest plan is to store rainwater from the roof, which is about pH 5.75, and when it is used up to fall back on mains water.

Under glass, or on a standing-out ground, plants in plastic pots can be sub-irrigated. A plastic sheet is laid flat with the edges turned up over boards or bricks to allow 2 inches (5 cm) of building sand to be spread over the sheet, the pots are stood on it and gently pressed in to make contact. Water is then trickled into the sand, or a more sophisticated tank and ball-valve can be installed, to maintain the water level. Some such device is invaluable in a holiday period. The plants take up water by capillary action from the sand-bed. It is possible to buy capillary mats which work as efficiently as sand-beds and can be moved around more easily.

FEEDING

Camellias in pots should be fed between April and July inclusive. The simplest method is to mix the feed with water; when watering on a small scale this can be done with a watering can. For a collection of plants a feed-bottle with a dilutor can be attached to the hose-pipe. Most shops sell several solid and liquid feeds.

The proportions of nitrogen (N), phosphate (P) and potash (K) vary in the feeds available. The analysis is printed on the label.

'Cornish Spring', a neat *cuspidata* hybrid which can be recommended for tubs

Choose one high in N for April, May and June, and one low in N and high in P and K for July, following the directions for dilution. If the label states that the N is ammoniacal nitrogen, that is a preferable feed. After July stop feeding. Some of the feeds contain trace elements. For camellias in pots, especially those in a peat-sand compost, it is an advantage to use such a feed for at least part of the season. Sequestrene is of no value to camellias in pots. *Reticulata* camellias require less feeding. Stop at the end of July and start again in April.

If a camellia is fed after August, when it is becoming inactive, a salt concentration will build up in the compost. If the first sign of this is a lining of white or brown powder edging the leaves, it may not be too late to soak the salts out of the compost and quickly re-pot. Then keep the roots on the dry side, damping over the leaves. Once the leaves turn brown and yellow and drop off, the roots will already have rotted and the plant will die.

A neglected plant usually has a poor root system. After re-potting and while it is being nursed back to health, it can be helped by spraying the leaves with a foliar feed, which is a dilute solution of fertilizer devised for this purpose. Similarly rooted cuttings in a sterile medium awaiting potting can be fed in this way. Such solutions provide a readily available form of nutrients for quick uptake by the leaves.

Propagation

CUTTINGS

Cuttings of most camellias root readily. A few, such as 'Augusto L. de Gouviea Pinto', will root but refuse to grow on and have to be grafted (see p. 41).

To be sure of success with cuttings bottom-heat (i.e. heating the rooting medium) is necessary, although a proportion will root without. Small propagation outfits are available to amateurs, usually consisting of a glass or 'Perspex' frame or miniature greenhouse with an insulated bed over a controlled heating device to supply bottom-heat, and a mist-nozzle above, all to be plugged in to the ordinary electric circuit and connected to a piped water supply.

It is feasible to rig up a tray of wet sand over a radiator or hot pipe and stand pots on it with cuttings in them and polythene bags over them. However, it is also possible to root camellia cuttings outdoors in the shade of a north wall with none of these devices.

Many camellias have a short resting period in late July or early August, when the first growth stops and hardens before either extending into secondary growth or making flower-buds. This period, when the sun heat can be used in a small greenhouse to assist rooting, is the best time to take cuttings. Those taken between October and February take longer to root.

Any shoot of the current year's growth, with four leaves or more, will do. Short shoots can be used for tip cuttings. Long shoots can be cut, with knife or secateurs, to provide one tip cutting and stem cuttings, each with three leaves. Cut or pull off the bottom leaf or two leaves and shave off an inch (2.5 cm) sliver of stem from the side opposite the basal bud. It is tidy, but not necessary, to trim the cutting across just below this bud.

When a stout growth with obvious plump buds is available, it can be made into single bud cuttings. After taking off the terminal cutting and a length at the bottom with small buds, which can be used for ordinary cuttings, a cut is made across above each big bud, so getting a number of short pegs of wood each topped by a leaf and bud. Cut the sliver down each peg.

After making the cuttings dip them in a hardwood rooting powder or liquid. (This is stronger than the material for soft green cuttings). The leaves may be cut in half to get more cuttings in the space but this is not desirable and certainly not necessary.

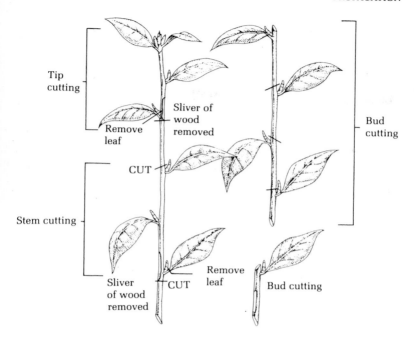

Figure 3: propagation by cuttings

Cuttings are rooted in a mixture of 75% peat and 25% grit; the grit must be lime-free, and it is probably easier to buy the small quantities required of alternative manufactured preparations instead. These are horticultural vermiculite, perlite, and polystyrene granules, each used with an equal volume of peat or finely ground fir-bark.

Prepare the chosen mixture, wet it well, and fill the bed of the propagator. If cuttings from other plants which may root at different times are also being put in, it may be simpler to root the camellias in pots. These should be filled with the mixture and shaken level without pressing down. Push the cuttings in up to the first leaf and water in well. If no mist propagator is available, cover with a thin grade polythene bag over the top of the pot or pulled over two crossing wires bent to make a dome shape with their ends pushed into the compost. Seal the polythene round the pot rim with a rubber band. A glass or plastic sweet jar can also be used, simply pushed down into the compost. Each week check that the bottom-heat is not drying out the compost down below. Water, if necessary, with warm water.

'Alba Plena', one of the oldest *japonicas*, was imported from China in 1792

Rooting should take place in 6 to 12 weeks, according to the time of year and the quality of the equipment used, after which the cuttings must be hardened off ready for potting. Those in a mist propagator will have the mist diminished or turned off and may then need shading. Those in polythene covered pots must be shaded anyway and are hardened by taking off the rubber band to let in air gradually. Those under a sweet jar should have the jar lifted and a finger-hole made under the rim to let in air for a week or two before removing the jar.

Reticulata camellias are usually the earliest to ripen their wood in July but take longer to root and, like cherries and magnolias, are most easily lost in the move for potting up. They make fewer roots and do not take kindly to disturbance. It pays to root single cuttings each in a 3-inch (7.5 cm) pot and to move them on into 5-inch (12.5 cm) pots in spring.

Cuttings taken in July are usually ready to pot in autumn; those taken in late autumn or winter may be left to be potted up in May or June by which time there may be a pretty big root system. Choose the size of pot which just fits the root spread without curling up the roots or tucking them in. The essential point now is that the young plant must not be potted too deeply. It should end up no deeper than it was in the rooting compost.

Put some compost in the bottom of the pot and with the other hand hold the plant over it with the roots almost resting on the compost. Fill in with compost round the roots to the top of the pot. With the tips of two fingers of each hand on either side of the stem gently press down the compost, give the pot a good tap on the bench and level off if necessary. With a bit of judgement it will end

'Captain Rawes', introduced in 1820, is still the commonest *reticulata* camellia in Britain

up with the top of the compost level with the bottom of the rim and the previous compost level mark on the stem. It is important not to firm the compost too much; it should just nicely hold together when the pot is turned over and the contents tapped out into the palm of the hand.

Water the pot and then keep it just damp in a shaded place. Resist the urge to over-water. Just damping over is better until the roots have got a good hold. If potted into a 3- or 3½-inch pot and kept under cover a plant will need potting on into a 5- or 6-inch pot next year.

GRAFTING

Grafting is relevant only to the amateur who may have a plant of a variety he wants to discard, or surplus plants from cuttings or some seedlings. It is best done in February.

This is when leaf-mottle virus is important (see p. 59). Seedlings will be free of it but if the unwanted variety has a Japanese name or origin or is an old Chinese variety like 'Alba Plena' it is almost certain to contain the virus. It may not show on the plant but will show up on scions grafted on it.

The grafting process is quite simple. Cut the stock plant off 2 or 3 inches (5–7.5 cm) from the roots using secateurs and then trim the cut with a sharp knife. Hold the knife over the centre of the cut and press it down to split the stock. If it is too tough for this, take an old thin table-knife and tap it down with a hammer to make the split. Cut a scion just like a cutting but from the middle or base of a strong firm young growth and, instead of cutting a sliver off it, use

41

a very sharp knife to trim it into a long wedge thin enough to fit tightly into the split stock but firm enough not to fray. Push the wedge in on one side of the split so that the bark of the stock and the scion meet each other and stay put. If the stock is a thick one, it may be necessary to hold the cut open by pushing in a screwdriver to hold it while the scion is being inserted. Tie the stock round with raffia, grafting tape or a plastic strip. It need not be waxed over but this is neater: a wad of sphagnum moss over the cuts helps the union of stock and scion.

Put a thin layer of fine damp sand over the compost around the stock and press the rim of a plastic or glass jar down into it to shut out air and retain moisture. Put in a shaded place.

One most important point is that the stock, if in a pot, must be well on the dry side before grafting to slow down the pressure of sap and it must not be watered until there are signs of growth on the scion. Even then, water sparingly. At this stage insert a finger under the rim of the jar to let in a little air. When the growth looks reliable, ease up the jar for a while and on a dull day take it off. If the growth wilts, put it back on and wean it a little longer, keeping it shaded.

Camellias rarely sucker but stocks do when cut back hard; all shoots below the union must be pulled off or cut close in with a sharp knife as soon as seen. Aphids too must be watched for: a soft shoot from the scion is appetising in March!

SEEDS

The apple-shaped fruits of camellias may contain fertile seeds, which ripen in late autumn, and should be sown immediately. The heaviest fruiter, 'Adolphe Audusson', is usually infertile.

Place the seeds in damp chopped sphagnum moss, or peat, in a polythene bag, tie it, and put it in the airing cupboard. The seeds will germinate in 6 to 8 weeks, and the young seedlings can then be seen in the bag.

When the roots are 3 inches (7.5 cm) long, carefully extract each seedling from the moss, cut off a third of the root and pot up in a 3-inch (7.5 cm) pot in a lime-free compost, with the seed only just covered. Slowly a shoot will grow and the first leaves expand. Keep in a mouse-proof place, e.g. a tray on top of glass jars. Grow on as for cuttings and allow five years to flowering.

Some camellias, such as *C. tricolor*, come nearly true from seed but the chance of getting a camellia worth naming is 1 in 10,000.

Camellia species and hybrids

SPECIES

All the camellia species grow wild in Asia, mostly in China, Japan and Indo-China, Burma and India. One of the results of their being collected originally by surgeon-botanists and missionaries was that only the dried specimens reached Europe. When a lucrative trade in plants did develop, it was naturally in the more flamboyant flowers grown by nurserymen near the treaty ports, whereas the small-flowered species remained as dried specimens. *Camellia kissii* exemplifies the attitude. Being a native of Nepal, it was collected early in the last century and grown for a short period but then allowed to die out. As a herbarium specimen it has been in Britain for a hundred years. Now it is again available live and has considerable promise. It suits the modern tendency away from the regular colourful flowers, which have got bigger and bigger, towards the light and graceful flowers of the species, and hybrids between them, notably in the Antipodes. In Britain most of the species require greenhouse cultivation and, although they flower when young, they become small trees.

Hybridists play a large part in the USA, which has the great advantage over Britain of a more liberal policy through the Plant Introduction Section of the US Department of Agriculture. This not only scours the world for every plant known, but examines, and in the case of camellias, develops their potential for wider cultivation and adaptation by breeding to suit the climate.

Current work on *C. oleifera* is an example of this. A succession of severe winters in the USA revealed that some strains of *C. oleifera* are the hardiest camellias known. Dr Ackerman of the US Department of Agriculture set out to produce coloured hybrids and some are now available. The species itself is grown over much of the southern half of China for the tea oil in its seeds. In Britain it has the disadvantage that it is autumn-flowering and its quite large, flat, white, single flowers are not borne on young plants. But the flowers have a sweet fragrance which is well dispersed. This species has been, and still is in many nurseries, confused with *C. sasanqua* 'Narumi-gata', which is distinguished by its cup-shaped white flowers having a touch of pink.

There are many attractive varieties of *C. sasanqua* with flower colours ranging from white through pink to almost red, plus bicolours, in varying forms and habits of growth. They are much used

Camellia chrysantha, the first yellow camellia to flower in the west, in the early 1980s

in Australia for espaliers and hedges. They like plenty of sun and are tolerant of a neutral or slightly alkaline soil; they can also be grown indoors (see p. 22). Their disadvantage in Britain is that, in an open situation outdoors, the flowers are pulped by a few degrees of frost in November and December.

Camellia japonica itself is a red single and good forms can be selected from its variable seedlings. The mountain forms, in Japan wintering under deep snow, are called rusticana camellias.

Captain Rawes, who brought from China the *reticulata* camellia named after him, also brought *C. maliflora*, a small double pink with profuse flowers resembling those of *Prunus triloba*, obviously a hybrid of unknown ancestry. It may be seen growing on a wall at Kew.

There are a few species hardy enough for Cornwall and southern Ireland – the tea plant, *C. sinensis*, a stiff round bush with nodding white flowers; two other whites, *C. tsaii* and *C. taliensis*, both winter-flowering, graceful and quite tall; and *C. granthamiana*, with big white single flowers, opening from dead-looking papery buds in late winter. It grows on the cool north side of a mountain above Hong Kong. The others on the borderline are *C. reticulata* itself, which has grown some 20 to 30 ft (6–9 m) high at Trewithen in Cornwall, with large single pink flowers; and *C. pitardii*, closely related to it.

The yellow-flowered camellias have been dealt with in the introduction (p. 10). Let us go on to the small-flowered species, several of which have fragrance. In size of flower smallness is dominant when they are hybridised. *Camellia rosaeflora* has small single pink flowers and has given rise to plants valuable for hanging baskets. *Camellia fraterna* is also graceful with white fragrant flowers and a hybrid, 'Tiny Princess', is very nearly hardy in Britain. The parent of 'Fragrant Pink', quite hardy in sun in Cornwall, and of other scented camellias, is *C. lutchuensis* from Okinawa Island. *Camellia kissii* has been mentioned and it also is fragrant. With similar charming white flowers en masse, *C. grijsii* is available in two forms, the typical one with rounded petals, its scented flowers as free as a briar rose, and the form known as *yuhsienensis*, with more widely spaced petals with deep serrations, reputedly more fragrant. *Camellia salicifolia*, also with white fragrant flowers, is in this country too.

The two species of major importance in Britain are *C. saluenensis* (see p. 9), a wide-spreading bush with narrow leaves and single flowers the size of a dog rose, ranging from white through puce to apple-blossom pink, and *C. cuspidata*, a rather straggly bush with narrow bronze leaves and small white flowers. It is the offspring of these two species which really matter in Britain,

Camellia granthamiana was discovered as recently as 1955, from a single tree growing in Hong Kong

together with those of *C. reticulata*, which have the largest flowers in the genus.

HYBRIDS

About twelve thousand varieties of *Camellia japonica* are known to exist. Assuming that ten thousand produce pollen to put on flowers of *C. saluenensis* they can give rise to, say, thirty thousand hybrids, some good, some bad, many indifferent, and a few superb. *Camellia Nomenclature* lists well over a hundred of these *williamsii* hybrids plus some derivatives. One such hybrid is 'Donation'.

The same process can be followed using *C. cuspidata* in place of *C. saluenensis*. There are only nine offspring listed.

This gives a glimpse of the potential for raising hybrids, first revealed by J.C. Williams at Caerhays Castle in Cornwall raising hybrids such as his namesake, a single pink, and 'George Blandford', a peony form pink from *C. saluenensis* pollinated by 'Akashigata' ('Lady Clare'), and by Colonel Stephenson Clarke crossing *C. saluenensis* with the *japonica* 'Masayoshi' ('Donckelaeri') to produce 'Donation'. All such hybrids between *C. saluenensis* and *C. japonica* are, with their offspring, known as *williamsii* hybrids in honour of J.C. Williams. Professor E.G. Waterhouse is commemorated by the hybrid named after him, the most distinctive of a group of seedlings he raised in Australia, but it was Les Jury in New Zealand who really raised the standard with 'Anticipation', 'Debbie', 'Elsie Jury', 'Elegant Beauty' and others, which join 'Donation' in pre-eminence in Britain where, generally, their quality is higher than in warmer countries.

One curious and valuable fact emerges – that the *williamsii* hybrids are hardier than their parents, first in forming flower buds and secondly, but slightly, in frost resistance. The same applies to *C. cuspidata*, itself not an ironclad. Crossed with *C. saluenensis* the offspring, 'Cornish Snow', is a very hardy floriferous white. 'Spring Festival', derived from *C. cuspidata* crossed with a big formal double, 'Sawada's Dream', is proving very hardy indeed and it has a most useful habit of growth.

The potential of *C. cuspidata* has not been fully realised nor exploited, possibly because of the dominance of big flowers until recently. In the USA Dr Ackerman in the US Department of Agriculture and Dr Clifford Parks in North Carolina University have hybridised nearly all the species available to identify their potential. Dr Ackerman led the field in the raising of fragrant camellias with 'Fragrant Pink' and others.

'Inspiration' (left), raised at Exbury, Hampshire, was judged the hardiest camellia at the International Camellia Trials in Britain; 'Water Lily' (right), a lovely *williamsii* hybrid from New Zealand

There are many desirable objectives in breeding camellias for Britain, not all the same as in the USA – for example, flowers that shatter when over, which is anathema where petal blight exists as in parts of the USA and Japan, but welcome here where a damp climate causes browning of petals and bushes have to be groomed. We look for the white which does not brown, red *williamsii* hybrids, small bushes, a scent which spreads, and so on, but hardiness and quality are paramount. In the transmission of hardiness, *C. japonica* prevails over tender *C. lutchuensis* in 'Fragrant Pink', *C. saluenensis* over *C. reticulata* in the very hardy 'Leonard Messel' and in 'Francie L', and *C. sasanqua* over *C. reticulata* in 'Flower Girl', 'Dream Girl' and 'Show Girl'. What has not been followed up is the hardiness inherent in hybrids which have forms of *C. reticulata* as the pollen parent. 'Inspiration' is the finest example with *C. saluenensis* as seed parent, also 'Dr Louis Pollizzi', 'Innovation' and 'Salutation'. "The Girls" were bred from a *sasanqua* seed parent with *reticulata* pollen parents. We do not know to what extent this increase in hardiness may be achieved in hybrids with the species *kissii*, *grijsii* and others which are on the borderline of hardiness in Britain.

It is not always the big organisation or the full-time researcher which breeds the successful hybrids. It is solely the province of amateurs in Britain, and amateurs in Australia and New Zealand have bred unusual hybrids which could be valuable in British greenhouses – 'Baby Bear' and 'Baby Willow', compact miniatures from *C. rosaeflora* × *C. tsaii*; 'Snowdrop' from *C. pitardii* × *C. fraterna*; 'Wirlinga Gem', 'Wirlinga Belle' and 'Wirlinga Princess', using *C. rosaeflora* with 'Tiny Princess' involving *C. fraterna* and *C. japonica*. It may be that camellias suitable for use as house plants will be found among hybrids between the less hardy species.

The seedlings derived from the Kunming forms of *C. reticulata*, now being introduced excessively in the USA, are greenhouse plants in most of Britain. Crossing with *japonica* varieties has not greatly increased their range beyond Cornwall and, perhaps, London.

BREEDING NEW CAMELLIAS

Australia, New Zealand, Japan, China, and California have the advantage that camellias seed freely and can be crossed outdoors. Pollination requires a temperature of 60°F (15.5°C) and this, in most of Europe, entails greenhouse cover. Miss Carlyon, at Tregrehan in Cornwall, used the device of an electric light bulb in a polythene bag around the flowers to raise the temperature for the selected bloom economically.

The opening flower will have petals closed around a central ovary or seed-vessel surrounded by stamens, each terminating in the male pollen-bearing anthers. The ovary has either a single style terminating in 3 or 5 arms or 3 to 5 separate styles. Each style ends in a stigma, the surface of which receives the pollen grains. The successful grain grows a pollen tube down the style to reach the ovary and fertilise the flower. Each flower can produce up to 3 or 5 seeds.

Decide which camellias are to be used as seed and pollen parents, endeavouring to ensure that they will flower simultaneously. Take the seed parent into a greenhouse to flower. When the selected flower begins to open cut away the anthers to prevent self-fertilisation. Within three days of the flower opening the stigmas become moist and are then ready to receive the pollen from the ripe anthers of the selected male parent. The pollen can either be brushed on the stigmas with a camel hair brush or a ripe anther used to touch gently each stigma. The flower has to be protected from alien pollination by enclosing it in a polythene bag or by putting the whole plant in an insect-proof cage. An American lady simplifies the process by segregating the style in a section of a large diameter drinking straw, sealing off the top with a gelatine capsule. Tie a tag label on the flower-stalk, recording the date, name of the pollen parent and so on. If successful, collect the ripe seed in the autumn and sow it (see p. 42).

A selection of camellia cultivars and hybrids

Recommending a camellia is a grave responsibility! Just as the supply of groceries is dominated by the chain stores so the choice of camellias tends to be decided by the garden centres. They have progressed from the bottom level of small unnamed plants in four colours to a high level of quality and a choice of, perhaps, ten or twenty varieties. The pacemaker, 'Donation', has established the era of new camellias and led on to the dominance of modern varieties easy to produce in quantity and sell as bushy well-budded plants. The influence of garden centres has spread far and wide so fast that the lists of the old traditional Cornish gardens and the Surrey nurseries have changed radically within the last ten years. But the upper level of twenty varieties still gives a very limited choice, bearing in mind that there are six classified flower forms and four main colour groups. It is unlikely that the purchaser of this handbook will remain a one-plant person for long or resist the urge to go for something different!

The lists which follow open the way to a wider choice, omitting some good old camellias which are no longer available, retaining others the excellence of which persists over many decades, and bringing in newer varieties which have been grown long enough to prove their special qualities and hardiness. It takes about six years to test a new introduction from abroad. Its performance under glass may conform but it may be quite different outdoors in Britain.

The lists here have been compiled in four specific sections – *williamsii* and allied hybrids; *japonica* cultivars; *reticulata* cultivars and hybrids; and *sasanqua* cultivars. The first two sections are divided into four main colour groups within which the cultivars are listed alphabetically. There are subsidiary lists to assist in garden use.

Note: the following name changes have been made for *japonica* camellias: 'Apollo' = 'Paul's Apollo'; 'Contessa Lavinia Maggi' = 'Lavinia Maggi'; 'Donckelaeri' = 'Masayoshi'; 'Jupiter' = 'Paul's Jupiter'; 'Lady Clare' = 'Akashigata'; 'Magnoliiflora' = 'Hagoromo'; 'Mathotiana Rubra' = 'Julia Drayton'; 'Nagasaki' = 'Mikenjaku'; 'Pink Perfection' = 'Otome'.

CLASSIFICATION OF FLOWERS

In order to simplify descriptions the different forms of flowers have been classified. *Camellia Nomenclature*, published by the Southern California Camellia Society and adopted by the American Camellia Society, gives six different classes with one sub-division and this is followed here, slightly abbreviated. The word petalode, or petaloid, is used to indicate stamens transformed into miniature petals.

Single. (S)   One row of not more than eight petals surrounding conspicuous stamens.
Semi-double. (SD)   Two or more rows of regular, irregular, or loose petals with conspicuous stamens.
Anemone form. (A)   One or more rows of large outer petals: the centre a mass of intermingled petalodes and stamens.
Peony form. (P)   Subdivided into:
Loose peony. (LP)   Loose petals which may be irregular, and intermingled stamens with, sometimes, intermingled petals, petalodes and stamens in centre.
Full peony. (P)   A convex mass of mixed irregular petals, petalodes and stamens, or irregular petals and petalodes not showing stamens.
Rose form double. (RFD)   Imbricated petals showing stamens in a concave centre when fully opened.
Formal double.   (FD)   Many rows of petals, fully imbricated, never showing stamens.

A different classification is followed in the Antipodes where anemone form becomes 'incomplete double or double centre' and peony form is 'informal double'.

Abbreviations at the end of each description denote flowering seasons: early (E), January onwards; mid (M), March onwards; late (L), April onwards.

WILLIAMSII AND ALLIED HYBRIDS

Hardy, most free-flowering camellias, mainly with smaller leaves than the *japonicas*.

White to yellow

Cornish Snow.   The best white for landscape planting, small flowers, very early, weathering better than others. Wide bush with coppery leaves. E–L.
E. T. R. Carlyon.   Strong grower, spreading, fine loose peony to rose form double flowers. M–L.
Jury's Yellow.   Upright habit, very prolific with medium anemone flowers, cream outer petals, pale yellow petaloids. Hardy. M.
Shiro Wabisuke.   An oddity of unknown origin with small fragrant flowers spaced among glossy narrow leaves through most of winter. Very hardy. Spent flowers drop off. E–M.

Pink to crimson

Anticipation.   Crimson rose, closely upright, large and prolific. Peony. M–L.
Ballet Queen.   Salmon pink, prolific, upright. Anemone. M–L.
Bow Bells.   Compact, bell-shaped pink. Single. Very early to late.
Bowen Bryant.   Large pink open bells; upright wide bush. Semi-double. M–L.

Williamsii and allied hybrids – 'Jury's Yellow (left), 'Dream Boat' (right)

Brigadoon. Rose-pink with broad petals; open habit. Semi-double. E–L. (See p. 26.)

Charles Colbert. Pale pink, prolific, semi-double flowers shatter when spent; upright bush. M–L.

Cornish Spring (*C. cuspidata* × *japonica*). Small dusky pink trumpets; compact, matt green leaves. Single. M–L. (See p. 37.)

Dainty Dale. Shaded orchid pink; upright, bushy, good in midlands. Peony. M–L.

Debbie. Blue-pink, deep regular flower, drops when over. Peony. E–L. (See p. 9.)

Donation. Compact to about 8 ft (2.4 m) wide when 15 ft (4.5 m) high; massed light pink flowers. Semi-double. M–L. (See p. 2.)

Dr Louis Pollizzi. Pale pink loose peony; very hardy. M–L.

Dream Boat. Clear pink, large formal double flowers, shatter when over. M–L.

Dream Girl. With 'Flower Girl' and 'Show Girl', hardy pinks with large flowers, strongly scented under glass. Semi-double. December to March.

E. G. Waterhouse. Close erect bush, pink flowers shatter when over. Formal double. M. (See p. 19.)

Elegant Beauty. Large deep rose, arching growths. Anemone to peony. M–L.

Elsie Jury. Large orchid pink, upright. Anemone, varies to peony form. M–L.

Francie L. (*C. reticulata* × *saluenensis*). Large deep rose, rich stamens; long dark leaves. Best for training on walls. Semi-double. (See p. 19.)

Garden Glory. Orchid pink; bushy, very early. Formal double. E–L.

George Blandford. Like its parent 'Lady Clare'; forms a wide bush. Peony. E–L.

Innovation. Wine red; makes a wide bush. Very hardy. Peony. E–L.

Inspiration. Brighter than 'Donation', better spaced flowers, same size bush. Semi-double. E–L. (See p. 47.)

J. C. Williams. Dog-rose pink, early. Long arching growths; good for north walls. Single. E–L.

Joan Trehane. Upright, large rose pink. Rose form double. L. (See p. 52.)

Julia Hamiter. Flesh pink on white, seedling of 'Donation', spreading bush, requires sun. Peony. M–L.

Laura Boscawen. Deep rose-pink, very free flowering, bushy. Anemone. M. (See p. 52.)

Leonard Messel. Loose peony, apricot-toned pink; very hardy. M–L. (See p. 14.)

Mary Larcom. Large, firm flowers and broad leaves. Single. M–L.

Mildred Veitch. Charming neat pink, does not shed dead flowers. Anemone. M.

November Pink. Thin arching branches loaded with single pink flowers November to May.

'Joan Trehane' (left), 'Laura Boscawen' (right)

Rose Parade. Dark crimson-rose, varies to formal double; makes open bush. Very hardy. Peony. M.

Senorita. Rose pink, neat deep flower; upright grower. Peony. L.

Spring Festival (*cuspidata* hybrid). Closely erect, small double pink flowers, coppery foliage. Formal double. L.

St Ewe. Early large dark pink funnels, glossy leaves. Single. E–M.

Water Lily. Sister seedling to 'Dream Boat', slender upright, flowers lavender tinted pink. Formal double. M–L. (See p. 47.)

Bicolor

Galaxie. Prolific formal double pink with red stripes. M–L.

Red

Black Lace. Perfect formal double dark red, medium size, but not precocious (i.e. does not flower when young – the death knell of many new camellias). M.

Freedom Bell. Medium semi-double, bright rather orange red, prolific dense *williamsii* bush. E–M.

Satan's Robe. Brilliant red semi-double; slender growths, *japonica* leaves, half *reticulata*, quarter *saluenensis*; hardy. M–L.

JAPONICA CULTIVARS

Broad-leaved traditional camellias, hardy but flowers decreasing in size from the midlands northwards and of little value in Scotland.

White

Alba Simplex. Large flat flowers. Single. M–L.

Campsii Alba. Old, small, very early, weathers well. Anemone. E–M.

Commander Mulroy. Very bushy, pink tinted buds, shatters when over. Formal double. M.

Haku-rakuten. Upright with irregular petals. Peony. M.

'Black Lace' (left), 'Satan's Robe' (right)

Janet Waterhouse. Glossy dark foliage, compact. Formal double. M.
Lily Pons. Distinctive long petals; weathers well. Semi-double. M.
Lovelight. Bold heavy trumpets and foliage. Semi-double. M.
Mary Costa. Informal anemone with full white centre. (See p. 54.)
Miss Universe. Spreading, late. Formal double. L.
Mme Charles Blard. Full peony. M.
Nobilissima. Often out before Christmas. Peony. E–M.
Primavera. Strong satisfactory rose form double. M.
White Nun. Spreading bush with very large flowers. Semi-double. M.

Pink to crimson

Akashigata ('Lady Clare'). Spreader with large leaves, salmon-pink variable flowers. Semi-double. M.
Berenice Boddy. Slender grower, medium size, two shades of pink. Semi-double. E–L.
Cheryl Lynn. Sugar-pink, shatters when over. Spreading. Formal double. M.
Debutante. Creamy pink, neat parent of 'Debbie'. Peony. M.
Edith Linton. Silvery pink. Rose form. M–L.
Elegans. Introduced in 1831 and still very much alive. FCC 1958. Anemone. M. (See p. 6.)
Gloire de Nantes. Rose-red semi-double to peony, often flowers in November. E–L.
Guilio Nuccio. Bold salmon red. Semi-double. M.
Hagoromo ('Magnoliiflora'). Blush medium flowers and growth, graceful. Semi-double. M. (See p. 13.)
Hana-tachibana. Bright reddish pink, late, compact. Formal double. L.
Julia Drayton ('Mathotiana Rubra'). Purple large flowers and large leaves. Rose form. L.
Laurie Bray. Soft pink bushy and prolific. Peony. M.
Otome ('Pink Perfection', 'Frau Minna Seidel'). Medium pale pink. Formal double. E–L.
Paul's Jupiter ('Jupiter'). Reliable, carmine-red. Single. M.
R. L. Wheeler Obese rose-pink, good variable form, open growth, stiff. Anemone. M.

Rubescens Major. Bold rose-red, broad leaves. Formal double. M. (See p. 23.)
Spencer's Pink. Upright and prolific. Single. M.
Sunset Glory. Coral-pink, large, retains its size in the midlands. Anemone. M.
Taro-an ('Yoibijin'). Pendent branches, glossy leaves, pale pink. Single flowers. E.
Tiffany. Shaded pink, spreading, not precocious. Peony. M–L.

Red

Adolphe Audusson. Bold red, uneven grower, many fruits but no seeds. Semi-double. M.
Alexander Hunter. Upright, fine stamens, crimson. Single. M.
Alice Wood. Large dusky dark red, not precocious but prolific when established, shatters when over. Formal double. L.
Australis. Bushy bright red. Peony. M.
Blaze of Glory. Open habit, broad leaves, blood-red, peony. M.
Bob Hope. Rich dark red semi-double to loose peony, bold dark green leaves. M–L.
Bob's Tinsie. Miniature anemone, leaves to match, boss of fine petaloids. M.
Cardinal's Cap. Close grower, bright red. Anemone. M.
C. M. Hovey. Dusky red, spreading. Formal double. M.
Coquetti ('Glen 40' in USA). Dark red, upright, not precocious. Formal double. M.
Dr Burnside. Close-growing, dark red peony. M. (See p. 35.)
Grand Prix. Classic beauty, big flat clear red, open wide grower. Semi-double. M–L. (See p. 61.)
Grand Slam. Large semi-double to peony or anemone form; bold foliage. M.
Konron Koku. Black red, semi-double to few petalled formal double. E–L.
Momiji-gari. Red 'Higo' with red filaments to stamens. Single. M.
Paul's Apollo ('Apollo'). Red. Robust, prolific, large, reliable. Semi-double. M.
Warrior. Dusky red, regular flat flower. Peony. M.

Bicolor

Bokuhan ('Tinsie' in USA). Small red with white boss, small leaves. Anemone. E.
Desire. The best of the popular formal doubles with white centre petals shading to three rows of deep pink. M.
Lady Loch. Dark pink edged white, loose peony. M–L.
Lavinia Maggi ('Contessa Lavinia Maggi'). Striped crimson, pink and white, Formal single. M.
Little Bit. Upright, small full red and white striped peony, sports red, large leaves. E–L.
Margaret Davis Picotee. White with a fine line of carmine edging. M.
Mikenjaku ('Nagasaki'). Blotched red and white. Semi-double. M.
Tricolor. Bushy, holly-like leaves, flowers with variable red and white stripes. Double. M. (See p.30).
William Bartlett. Compact, steady white powdered and lightly striped crimson. Formal double. M.
Yours Truly. Best sport of 'Lady Vansittart', crimson edged white. Semi-double. L.

Opposite: *japonicas* – 'Mary Costa', 'C. M. Hovey' (top left and right), 'Grand Slam', 'Paul's Apollo' (centre left and right), 'Warrior', 'William Bartlett' (bottom left and right)

Reticulatas – 'Arch of Triumph' (left), 'Lasca Beauty' (right)

RETICULATA CULTIVARS AND HYBRIDS

There are now many of these magnificent camellias, among which are the largest flowers in the genus, 7 inches (18 cm) or more in diameter. They generally require greenhouse space which limits the demand for them because their relatively sparse growth cannot be pruned heavily to make a dense bush. They can be grown successfully in London and much more widely than they are in Cornwall where their quality is magnificent. Out of over 200, here is a representative selection based on experience outdoors in Cornwall and under glass.

Arch of Triumph. Large peony with a bright orange sheen attracting attention to its crimson-rose flowers. E.
Captain Rawes. Semi-double rose-pink, one of the glories of the greenhouse at Chatsworth in April. M. (See p. 41.)
Dr Clifford Parks. Hybrid with *C. japonica*, full dark orange-red peony or anemone flowers. M.
Dream Castle. Enormous pale pink peony flowers, large leaves, open spreading branches. M.
Eden Roc. Classic semi-double pink, upright, with bold foliage. M.
Harold L. Paige. Very large peony flower, bright orange-red. L.
Interval. Flat semi-double pink increasing in size to 6 inches (15 cm) after opening. Modest space-user under glass. E.
Lasca Beauty. Hybrid with bold foliage and semi-double pink trumpets. M.
Lila Naff. Wide round bush with big pale pink cupped flowers, semi-double. L.
Mandalay Queen. Deep full rose peony flowers 7 inches (18 cm) across. M. (See p. 26.)
Miss Tulare. Bright red full regular peony. M.
Royalty. Finest semi-double red hybrid with curving branches, pendent in the open, good for training on walls. M–L. (See p. 17.)
Valentine Day. Formal double salmon-pink with sparse foliage. M–L.
William Hertrich. Prolific cherry-red, loose peony outdoors, semi-double under glass. M.

SASANQUA CULTIVARS

Autumn-flowering camellias, mostly scented, flowering very freely after a hot summer, liking more sun than *japonicas*, tolerant of less acid soils, and with leaves and flowers mostly smaller than those of *williamsii* hybrids. They do need warm positions sheltered from autumn frosts and some are easily trained on walls. Many varieties have been raised in Japan and, more recently, in Australia and the USA and, including the later forms sometimes classified as hiemalis camellias, some 228 are listed of which a useful fifteen are mentioned here.

Bettie Patricia. Large rose-form double, shell-pink.
Chansonette. Formal double or peony, wall plant.
Dazzler. Rose-red peony or semi-double, walls.
Exquisite. Large single pale pink, walls.
Hugh Evans. Prolific single pink, walls.
Jean May. Shell pink double.
Narumi-gata. Pink-tinted cupped single white, often sold as *C. oleifera*, walls.
Navajo. Rose-red with white centre, large semi-double, good hedger.
Plantation Pink. Large single pink, hedger.
Rainbow. Large single white with red border, strong.
Setsu-gekka. Large white semi-double with waved petals.
Showa-no-sakae. Soft pink rose-form or semi-double, low grower.

CAMELLIAS FOR SPECIAL PURPOSES

Walls

Facing south (partially shaded), west, east: 'Francie L', 'Dream Girl', 'Flower Girl', 'Show Girl', 'Daintiness', 'Mary Phoebe Taylor', 'November Pink', 'Elegant Beauty', 'Satan's Robe', 'Cornish Snow', *japonica* 'Grand Prix', *sasanquas* (as listed above).

Facing north: 'Elegant Beauty', 'J. C. Williams', 'Daintiness', 'November Pink' and, as free-standing bushes, 'Bow Bells', 'Donation', 'Inspiration', 'St Ewe', 'Debbie'.

The *japonica*, 'Shiro Chan'

Tubs (compact growers)

Japonicas: 'Australis', 'Bob's Tinsie', 'Cardinal's Cap', 'Cecile Brunazzi', 'Commander Mulroy', 'Debutante', 'Dr Burnside', 'Janet Waterhouse', 'Laurie Bray', 'Bob Hope', 'Wilamina', 'Ave Maria'.

Hybrids: 'Anticipation', 'Black Lace', 'Cornish Spring', 'Free Style', 'Wilber Foss', 'Spring Festival'.

Hardiness (as far north as Perth)

'Anticipation', 'Bowen Bryant', 'Brigadoon', 'Cornish Snow', 'Donation', 'Freedom Bell', 'Inspiration', 'J. C. Williams', 'Leonard Messel', 'St Ewe' and probably, 'Dr Louis Pollizzi', 'Free Style', 'Rose Parade', 'Senorita' and 'Spring Festival'.

Hedges See p. 29–30.

Greenhouses

Most of the *japonica* and hybrid camellias can be grown successfully in cold or temperate structures with glazing or polythene cladding. The form of flower may be different from outdoor flowers, sometimes to the extent of putting it in a different classification. Here are a few notable camellias which attract attention from people who have no greenhouse and disappoint when grown outdoors. (See also *reticulatas*, p. 56, species, p. 43 and p. 31.)

Berenice Perfection. A rich formal double in two shades of pink. Upright grower. M–L.

Elegans Champagne. White with a honey centre. Small and easily damaged outdoors.

Kramer's Supreme. A rich reddish pink peony which produces perfect flowers outdoors in December! In a greenhouse its form, colour and its carnation scent can be fully appreciated in a much greater display.

Mrs D. W. Davis. The badge of the International Camellia Society, almost useless outdoors in Britain but an enormous spectacular white under cover. (See p. 32.)

Nuccio's Gem. A spiral formation formal double white which is sparse in leaf and petal outdoors but outstanding under glass.

Shiro Chan. A perfect white anemone, sometimes with a little pink, under glass. Derived from 'Chandler's Elegans' as a mutation. (See p. 57.)

Souvenir de Bahuaud Litou. Raised in France in 1908 as a flesh-pink sport of 'Mathotiana Alba' which weathers so sadly that it deserves cover to perfect its beauty.

Tiny Princess. A quite distinct miniature hybrid between *C. fraterna* and *C. japonica* 'Akebono' with grace enough to tempt the outdoor grower but rewardingly different under glass.

Problems

The list in the following pages looks frightening but in practice camellias have few troubles and require no routine spraying, unless scale insects are around.

DISEASES

Variegations. The camellia grower, particularly the enthusiast with a greenhouse and a large collection, needs to be able to differentiate between harmless and infective types of variegation. It would be misleading to describe propagation by cuttings without a warning of the hazard. A narrow pale edging of the leaves of camellias with *saluenensis* parentage, particularly if growing in full sun, is the harmless effect of climate, probably extremes of night and day temperatures.

A pattern of variegation which is regular and consistent is of physiological or genetic origin, usually a harmless chimaera. The best known examples are 'Golden Spangles', a *williamsii* hybrid, and 'Reigyoku', a *japonica* (see p. 61). Branches which revert to green should be cut out. The camellia sold as 'Benten' has green and white small leaves.

The infective cause of variegation of leaves and flowers has in the past been called 'leaf mottle virus'. It is, however, not yet known whether the infective agent is a virus or a related organism, so it is safer to refer to it as a virus-like disease. It is transmissible by grafting. It is common practice in the USA to infect new camellias in order to get blotched flowers. Any name followed by 'Var' indicates such induced blotching. Stripes are not normally viroid.

Another source of infection is in most of the old Chinese and Japanese camellias such as 'Akashigata' ('Lady Clare'), 'Masayoshi' (Donckelaeri), 'Bokuhan', 'Ake-bono', and the Kunming *reticulatas*. The leaves may show yellow mottling, or spots, or be wholly yellow. The infection cannot be removed from the plant but it can be masked by the liberal use of sulphate of ammonia: 'R. L. Wheeler' responds well to this. 'Ake-bono' is a tolerant carrier which does not show infection. Silver flecking with distortion and reduction in size of leaf is a more dangerous form of this infection and plants showing these symptoms should be burnt.

Some virus-like infections are transmitted by insect, usually aphid, vectors sucking the sap and moving from plant to plant. In India, where the health of the leaves of the tea-plant is important economically, scientists have proved that leaf-mottle virus is transmitted by aphids on *C. sinensis* and *C. japonica* varieties. In my own experience the peach aphid, which is large and green, does transmit leaf-mottle virus. The early spring shoots of camellias in glass frames are soft and succulent and some 800 plants were infected by leaf-mottle from a known source of infection – a plant which should not have been there. Any camellia grower will be wise to take preventive measures to control aphids under glass (see opposite).

Leaf-gall (Exobasidium camelliae). This repulsive white jelly-like enlargement of the leaf or flower is seen more frequently on camellias nowadays. Removal of an infected leaf usually clears it but if it persists spray with mancozeb or a copper fungicide.

Stem wilt (Glomerella cingulata). This occurs under glass or polythene when the temperature and humidity are both too high. Leaves become blotched near the edges and twigs die back or the stem cankers. With good management, it should not arise. All that need be added is that in very hot humid spring weather in Cornwall this disease may affect *reticulata* camellias outdoors. The effect is generally no more than a reduction in the thickness, and browning, of the bent portion of the wilting stem.

Leaf spot (Pestalotiopsis guepini). This is associated with a very humid, airless environment. It shows as grey or brown spots on the leaves. Amateur gardeners are unlikely to encounter this disease unless they are growing camellias under cover where there is excessive humidity. Obviously cuttings taken from plants so grown and infected will get worse in the humidity of the propagation outfit and should be drenched with benomyl.

Honey fungus (Armillaria spp.). Camellias are not immune to this disease. It spreads, usually, from decaying wood upon which it feeds, from tree stumps and fallen branches. When it has reduced the wood to jelly it spreads just under the surface of uncultivated ground. Unfortunately in cultivated ground it may spread below the depth of the spade. Its long thick black rhizomorphs, like bootlaces, are easily seen and removed: the bright chestnut brown threads, which fan out in search of a host, are the lethal parts of the fungus.

Plants with a healthy root-system may tolerate the presence of the fungus unharmed, but as soon as damage is inflicted, maybe by drought, bad drainage, or wounding of the roots by cultivation, perhaps the removal of a perennial weed with a spade, or even an

'Reigyoku', (left), a chimaera, has a gold ostrich-feather pattern on the leaves; 'Grand Prix' (right), an excellent red *japonica* cultivar

insect bite, then the fine rhizomorphs enter the roots and kill. Although I have successfully cured an infected camellia of honey fungus, there is nothing approved for use against it under the current pesticides legislation.

PESTS

Camellias are not greatly troubled by pests, although there are some which may require control measures. Most insecticides can be used safely on camellias, provided they are not applied to the open flowers.

Aphids. Outdoors, these are usually brown and cluster thickly on young leaves, particularly on the secondary growths in late summer, causing leaf distortion. Spot control with an aerosol is usually sufficient but heavier infestations can be sprayed with pirimicarb, malathion, heptenophos or dimethoate.

   Under glass early young growths attract green aphids and later the brown aphids appear. Control by hanging dichlorvos vaporising strips is advisable or one of the above sprays can be used.

Scale insects. Two types may be found, soft scale and cushion scale. The case of the soft scale is up to $\frac{1}{8}$ inch (4 mm) long, half as wide, yellow-brown, fixed to the undersurface of the leaf. Cushion scale forms white woolly wads on the stems and also on the undersurface of the leaves. Control is by spraying with malathion or pirimiphos-methyl during late July and August when the more susceptible younger stages are present.

   Both scale insects and aphids can cause a sooty deposit on the upper surfaces of some leaves. This soot is a harmless mould, which can be wiped off, but it grows on the honeydew excreted by harmful insects such as aphids or scale insects feeding on the undersides of the leaves above.

Vine weevils. These have become a major pest in Cornwall and may be so elsewhere. The adults bit irregular notches in the leaf margins, especially on low-growing branches. The eggs may be laid in the soil outdoors and, more often, in the compost of pot plants and the white larvae then eat the roots away and ringbark the main stem, which later kills the camellia. Primulas especially attract them. Control is by drenching the roots of all pot plants in the greenhouse or standing ground with a solution of gamma-HCH. Dusts of gamma-HCH can be used to kill the adult weevils. The adults are grey-brown and active only at night when an inspection by torchlight may be profitable. All are female and, without benefit of matrimony, each may lay 500 eggs. A high standard of hygiene is advisable, clearing away all leaves and litter, and emptying pots, trays and packing materials, their normal hiding-places.

Birds. Early single or semi-double flowers, outdoors and under glass, are sometimes torn apart or disfigured by the claws of small birds, principally blue tits, as they seek the copious nectar at the base of the stamens. A proprietary bird-repellent based on aluminium ammonium suphate is effective if the bushes are sprayed as directed when the first flowers are open. Flower buds are sometimes taken by grey squirrels in cold weather and heaped on the ground for no good purpose.

Mice and voles. These may girdle the stem at ground level under snow, causing the bush to die slowly during the summer. Keep watch.

DISORDERS

Corky scab, oedema. This shows as linear brown excrescences, usually curved, on both surfaces of the leaf, more often the upper surface. It is thought to be a physiological reaction to humid conditions in the atmosphere or the soil. Well aerated and drained soil, a buoyant atmosphere under glass, and moderate balanced feeding, may prevent its occurrence. It appears to have no ill effects on the plant, however unsightly and worrying it looks. Do not remove affected leaves as that will make matters worse.

Algae. Under trees, especially pines, leaves may become encrusted with a fine grey-green deposit, difficult to remove. This is a harmless alga and a well-fed plant in the open will outgrow it.

Root strangulation. See p. 23.

Bud drop. The shedding of small immature buds in the winter may be a natural reduction of an excessive formation of multiple buds. When plump, apparently normal buds drop it is usually due to excessive feeding, feeding with nitrogen too late in the season, or a period of drought, perhaps, no more than a day or two during July, August or September during which the plant goes seriously short of water. Generally the more complicated the flower the more prone to bud-drop is the camellia. Keep a sharp eye on plants near dry corners of walls or in ground near greedy trees and hedges such as beech and privet.

Balling. In its dictionary meaning of 'clogging' this aptly fits a condition uncommon in Britain which occasionally occurs during a dry spring. In the USA it is due to dry heat but in New Zealand it is attributed to sun warming frosted flowers.

The tissues of outer petals become damaged in such a way as to form a dead sheath enfolding the inner petals and preventing their expansion. The bud swells but cannot open and eventually in the pressure developed all the unopened petals split from the stem at their base. By this time some rot has set in and can spread to adjacent buds and the damage becomes cumulative unless the balled flowers are pulled off. Balling was a serious problem in the spring of 1984. The cause was the many weeks of continuous drying east wind with cold nights and hot days with no rain for relief. As the old men would say 'The petals lost their nature'.

DIAGNOSIS

The following notes are intended to help the owner of an apparently ailing camellia to use the leaves as indicators of the identity of the ailment, to think about what may have been done, or left undone, which made the plant sick, and to decide what may restore it to health.

Yellow leaves, mostly the older ones, sometimes with the veins staying green: lack of water or fertilizer, or both. Feed is only taken up in solution.

Yellow and brown blotches on the leaves between the veins: soil conditions too alkaline. This often happens to camellias in pots when ordinary JI, rather than ericaceous, compost has been used (see p. 33).

Yellowing leaves with green leaves pale in colour hanging limp on a plant with poor anchorage: see honey fungus, p. 60.

Yellow and brown leaves with leaf-fall and loss of anchorage: see root strangulation, p. 23.

Mottled yellow leaves with perhaps some leaves wholly yellow, or merely a few yellow spots on one or two leaves: see variegation, p. 59.

Leaves speckled silver with reduction in size and distorted outlines: see variegation, p. 59.

Brown shading on leaf surface, showing on the curved part: leaf-scorch due to inadequate water and humus in a hot position.

Brown blisters through the leaves: sun scorch, too hot an exposure, or, in a greenhouse, lack of ventilation, shading, or humidity. Leaf spot looks similar but the brown patches are usually on plants already in poor condition in damp surroundings.

Brown edges with a pale, yellowing leaf surface: chemical imbalance, lime accessible to roots, excessive feed, animal manure, spreading soil over the roots. With leaf-drop under glass: feeding too late in the year, overwatering.

Purplish brown patches on the leaves: frost damage, after ice has formed in the leaf tissue.

White powder on leaf edges: excessive salts from chemical in soil e.g. from iron-impregnated ditch clearings, slurry.

Black sooty deposit: see aphids or scale insects, p. 61.

Brown excrescences: see corky scab, p. 62.

Grey-green encrustation: see algae, p. 62.

Useful organizations

International Camellia Society
UK membership: Geoffrey Yates, Stagshaw, Ambleside, Cumbria
  LA22 0HE
Channel Islands and Ireland: Mrs Ann Bushell, Lower Hall, Rue de
  la Pompe, Augres, Trinity, Jersey

American Camellia Society
UK: Mrs Mayda Reynolds, Westward, Le Marquanderie, St Brelade,
  Jersey

Southern California Camellia Society
PO Box 50525, Pasadena, California 91105, USA

New Zealand Camellia Society
J L Warsaw, PO Box 204, Wanganui, New Zealand

Rhododendron and Camellia Group of the Royal Horticultural Society
R H Redford, Fairbank, 34 Rectory Rd, Farnborough, Hants GU14 7BT